WRITIN STORIES

Rayne Hall

WRITING DARK STORIES

Copyright Rayne Hall © 2014
All Rights Reserved - content copyright Rayne Hall
Cover art and design by Erica Syverson
Scimitar Press (September 2014 Edition)

TABLE OF CONTENTS

INTRODUCTION - 6

1. FEED YOUR FICTION WITH YOUR FEARS - 8
Places. Weird Shudders. Phobias. Childhood Fears. Dreams. Human Attitudes. Ordinary Things. Assignment.

2. WHY THE TITLE IS A STRONG START - 13
Gathering Ideas. Assignment.

3. WRITING BY THE SEAT OF YOUR PANTS - 16
Now Write. Prompts. The Freewriting Experience. Assignment.

4. FIFTEEN MASTER PLOTS -19

5. DARK FICTION AND HORROR GENRES - 25
Horror. Splatterpunk. Extreme Horror. Psychological Horror. Dystopian. Lovecraftian. Thriller.
Mystery. Dark Fiction. Supernatural. Paranormal. Paranormal Romance. Dark Fantasy. Urban
Fantasy. Gothic. Erotic Horror. Horror Comedy. Romantic Suspense. Steampunk. Ghost Stories.
Slipstream. Speculative Fiction. Weird Fiction. Flash Fiction. Slice-of-Life. Cross-Genre.
Collection. Anthology. Assignment.

6. POINT OF VIEW - 33
Deep PoV Techniques. Serial Point of View. Omniscient Point of View. Other Point of View Styles.
Assignment.

7. MANAGING TENSION - 38

Goal. Raising the Stakes. Conflicts Among Characters. Peaks and Troughs. Assignment.

8. BUILDING SUSPENSE - 43
Pose a Question. The Ticking Clock. Pacing. The Door Opens. Assignment.

9. HOW TO SCARE YOUR READERS - 47
Darkness. Sounds. Chill. Isolation. Meet the Monster. Get Visceral. The Gory Bits. Assignment.

10. CREEPY LOCATIONS - 53
Select the Setting. Inspiring Pictures. How to Describe the Setting. Practical Research. Setting Research Checklist. Assignment.

11. MAKE THE MOST OF THE WEATHER - 60
Create Atmosphere. Deepen the PoV. Make it Difficult for the Characters. Strained Tempers. Mood and Foreboding. Beware the Pathetic Fallacy. Collecting Descriptions. Assignment.

12. HOW TO OPEN YOUR STORY - 64
Opening with Setting Description. Opening with Dialogue. Opening While All Seems Well with the World. Assignment.

13. HOW TO END YOUR STORY - 69
Endings to Avoid. Seven Possible Endings. Leave Questions in the Reader's Mind. Assignment.

14. VILLAINS AND MONSTERS - 72
Human Villains: Clichés to Avoid. Motivation. Depth. Describing the Villain. Monsters: Reveal it

Bit by Bit. Keep it Plausible. Assignment.

15. GHOST STORIES - 78
Plot and Backstory. Setting and Mood. Characters and Point of View. Assignment.

16. VAMPIRES, WEREWOLVES, ZOMBIES - 81
Vampires: Sparkling Versus Traditional. Vampire Tropes. Fiction Ideas. Werewolves: Werewolf Tropes. Questions to Consider. Zombies: How Zombies are Made. Zombie Tropes. Fiction Ideas. Beware the Bite-Hiders. Assignment.

17. RELIGIOUS HORROR - 91
Horror in Holy Books. Faith Versus Fear. Religious Historical Horror. Unbelievers Meet Scary Gods. Stories Presenting Religion as Evil. Writing About Other Faiths. Controversy. Assignment.

18. WHY DO PEOPLE READ HORROR FICTION? - 97
Seven Psychological Reasons. Assignment.

19. MARKETING AND PUBLICATION - 99
Traditional Publishing. Markets. Rights. Payment. Self-Publishing. Trends. Assignments.

20. SAMPLE STORIES WITH COMMENTS - 105
Burning. Seagulls. Only A Fool. The Devil You Know.

DEAR READER -136

ACKNOWLEDGEMENTS – 137

OTHER BOOKS IN THE SERIES - 138

Writing Dark Stories

INTRODUCTION

As a writer of dark short stories, you can entertain your readers and at the same time make them think.

This book gives you a wealth of plot ideas and techniques for creating powerful, provocative, chilling tales your readers won't forget.

Make their spines tingle with anticipation and their skins crawl with delicious fear. Disturb their world-view and invite them to look into the dark corners of their own souls.

'Dark Fiction' can mean three types of literature:

1. A synonym for 'Horror', the literature of fear. These stories aim to thrill with frights, allowing the readers to savour foreboding, suspense and terror from the safety of their armchairs.

2. Fiction exploring the nature of evil. Stories of this kind stretch the boundaries between good and bad. They challenge perceptions, provoke thoughts, and invite readers to probe their own consciences. These stories may be subtle, but they ask disturbing questions and can leave impressions the readers won't ever forget.

3. Paranormal fiction with dangerous elements. With an aim to entertain and excite, these stories offer the reader an escape from reality. Many feature vampires and werewolves, and they often involve a strong love story.

Your short stories may be one of these, a combination of two, or even all three.

All ideas, guidelines and techniques are suggestions, not rules, and not every chapter is relevant for every story. Choose the ones that fit the tale you want to tell. After all, you want to become known for your own distinct storytelling style, not as a clone of Rayne Hall. Adapt my techniques so they don't restrict your writing, but enrich it.

If you're new to the writing craft, you may want to put this book aside for now and start with a beginners' fiction writing guide. If you're an experienced author, you may already be familiar with some concepts. Feel free to skip those sections or to use them as a refresher.

For the examples I've used excerpts from my own stories, because I own the copyright to them. At the end of the book, I'll share four complete short stories, so you can see how I have applied those techniques.

In some sections, I use female pronouns, in others male. This is to avoid clunky constructions like 'He or she gives his or her thing to her or him'. Almost all suggestions in this book apply to either gender. The words, spelling, grammar and punctuation are British English.

Enjoy my book, create great stories, and give your readers something to think about.

Rayne Hall

CHAPTER 1: FEED YOUR FICTION WITH YOUR FEARS

Cowards make the best horror writers, because we know what fear feels like, and we never run out of ideas.

What frightens you? Fire, spiders, dentists' drills? Use these fears in your fiction and build your stories around them. Here are some ideas.

PLACES

Do you know any creepy places? Does the thought of certain dangerous locations make you queasy? Is there an abandoned building that gives you shudders each time you pass? Does a house in your neighbourhood ooze malevolence? Do you have to brace yourself each time you climb into your attic? Are you terrified of walking a certain path? Creepy places make atmospheric fiction settings. Many of my short stories started from descriptions of such locations. You can also use those places in your novels, especially for suspense-rich scenes or the book's climax.

'The Bridge Chamber' - probably the scariest of my stories – started with the uneasy memory of a railway bridge where I used to play as a child. The masonry was pierced with tunnels, just big enough for a child to squeeze through, and we dared one another to explore those dark dank spaces.

WEIRD SHUDDERS

Are you frightened of something that other people consider harmless? One of my friends can't bear the sight of long fingernails, and the sound of nails scraping on a surface sends her into a panic. Another fears moths and butterflies, especially when they get near her face. I also know a man who is terrified of clothing zips. He always wears buttoned garments, because he can't breathe when encased in zippered clothes. I also know people who get the creeps when they see a balloon, a clown's face or a peach.

If you have such a fear – whether it's a full-blown terror or just a shuddery feeling – write a short story about it. Since many things give me the creeps – garden slugs, crowded rooms, telephones, the whine of a dentist's drill – I've been able to write many stories about them. Stories inspired by weird fears often get published in anthologies.

PHOBIAS

Many people have phobias – fears about specific situations, so intense that they have a paralysing, crippling effect. Claustrophobia, the fear of enclosed spaces, is a common example. Often, these fears are based on a sensible, instinctive response to a genuine danger such as heights, caves, fire or snakes, and are irrational only in their strength. Others are less easy to explain. Some people get paralysed when crossing a bridge, others freak out when they hear the hissing noise of a not-quite-closed thermos flask.

If you have a phobia, I encourage you to write a story about it. Your story will have a level of authenticity that other writers can't achieve. However, writing about your phobia can be scary, and if it causes you more distress than you can bear, set it aside for a while until you feel strong enough to continue.

'Burning' - probably my best-known short story – started when I gathered my courage to address my fear of fire, a phobia that had tormented me all my life. Thinking about what fire meant to me and plotting the story was a frightening ordeal, but once I started putting my thoughts on paper and shaping them into fiction, I gained control over my fear. When the piece was complete, two amazing things happened: My phobia all but vanished, and the story won awards.

CHILDHOOD FEARS

What terrified you when you were a child? Whether the danger was real or imagined, your emotions were probably intense. What if there really was a cannibal living in your wardrobe or a dragon waiting behind the cellar door? Childhood fears can inspire awesome paranormal horror stories.

As a kid, I lived in a railway station where my father was station master, and I was terrified of the giant black steam engines that stopped outside our home to puff dark smoke and emit shrill whistles. When I had an idea for a ghost story and needed to up the creepiness, I placed the characters in an old railway tunnel with a thundering steam train.

DREAMS

Have you ever had a dream that left you disturbed? Do you have a recurring nightmare? If you dream about the same horror night after night, consider adapting it as a fiction plot.

Some of my most successful short stories stemmed from dreams, including 'The Painted Staircase'.

You may want to keep a notebook on your bedside table so you can write down your dreams immediately after waking, because dreams tend to fade from memory fast.

HUMAN ATTITUDES

What human behaviours and attitudes disturb or distress you? Lies? Cruelty? Wife-beating? Greed? Abuse of authority? Bullying? Unbending bureaucracy? People who shut their eyes and ears to the suffering of others? Use dark fiction to explore those issues. The resulting stories will have the disturbing depth and the power to make your readers think.

In many of my stories, you will find racism, religious fanaticism, prejudice, injustice and hypocrisy, either in the main plot or in the subtext.

ORDINARY THINGS

What's right before your eyes? Look at the ordinary objects on your desk, the landscape outside your window, the pets in your home. What if one of them is not as harmless as it seems, but is really an instrument of an evil power, or takes on a destructive entity? What could the printer, the coffee cup, the rag rug or the kitten develop into?

'Seagulls' - my most reprinted story – started with the seagulls that pecked at my window every morning. Such pretty animals, white-feathered, silver-tipped, with eyes like yellow haloes around death-dark cores. Surely they were harmless... but what if they were not?

ASSIGNMENT

Using these suggestion, make a list of everything that frightens you, used to frighten you, or might frighten you. Try to come up with at least twenty. My list has over two hundred items. Can you top that?

Rayne Hall

CHAPTER 2: WHY THE TITLE IS A STRONG START

As soon as you have a title that thrills you, the ideas will come. But it needs to be a title that resonates with you, not something that pleases only other people. It should make your stomach clench or your throat constrict, something that makes you nervous or eager to discover what the story is about.

GATHERING IDEAS

Where do you find such a title for your story? I recommend you pick a title before you even start writing. Create a whole list of titles, save it, and whenever you want to write the story, you select a title from your list.

I learnt this method from Ray Bradbury and it works a treat for me, especially for dark and scary yarns. Try it and see for yourself.

Look at the list you've created in the assignment for Chapter 1 – all the things that frighten or disturb you. Write each of them as a title, then tweak it to create variations.

The creative part of your psyche – otherwise known as 'The Inner Muse' or 'Artist Brain' loves this approach. Once it's in title-creating mode, it will come up with idea after idea.

Let's say you have a fear of dentists, and you find lies disturbing. Then your list might look like this:

The Dentist
Dentists
Dental Check-up
The Dentist's Revenge

The Dentist's Promise
A Tale of Two Dentists
The Third Dentist
Dental Treatment
In the Dentist's Chair
You Know The Drill
Death and the Dentist
The Tooth Must Come Out
Dental Dangers
Trust Me I'm A Dentist
Liar
The Liars
Lies
Three Lies
Four Liars
The Second Lie
Lie To Me
She Lied
No Lies
What Lie
The Lying Dentist
The Dentist's Lie
The Dentist Who Lied
and so on.

You can come up with dozens of great titles, and each of them will be perfect for your writing.

Once your Artist Brain is in title-creating mode, it may not want to stop. Evocative titles will flash through your mind while you peel the potatoes or drive down the motorway. Keep a notebook at hand and jot them down as soon as it is safe.

ASSIGNMENT

Make a list of titles, inspired by your answers in the Lesson 1 assignment. Make it as long as you can, perhaps coming back to it after a break. Keep this list on your computer or in a notebook where you can access it easily, because you will use it often.

CHAPTER 3: WRITING BY THE SEAT OF YOUR PANTS

Pick one of the titles from the list you've created – the one that thrills you and makes your fingers itch to dance across the keyboard.

NOW WRITE

Write whatever comes to your mind. Don't pause, just keep going. You can do this on the computer or by hand. I like doing it with coloured gel pens in lined hardback notebooks.

Jot down all the thoughts that come to your mind without pausing. Call up your memories of the dreams and events, evoke the emotions. This process is called freewriting.

The creative part of your psyche - Artist Brain – enjoys this approach. Don't revise, edit, or censor your writing. Just let it flow. When you're stuck, consider the title once more, and explore the topic from a new angle.

PROMPTS

Writing prompts help when the creative stream dries up. Pick one of these questions and write about it:

What feelings does this title rouse in me? Where in the body do I feel them? How?
Where do these feelings come from?
Have I experienced something like this?
Do I know of someone to whom this has happened?
What's the worst that could happen?
What kind of person might get into this situation?
How did my character get into this situation?

How can I make this situation even worse?
Why does the character do this?
What does the character need right now? Why?
What's the weirdest place where this story could unfold?
What's the weather like?
The main character is ignorant about something. What is it?
Why can't the main character take the obvious way out?
There's a door, wall or barrier somewhere. What's behind it?
What will happen if the character crosses this?
Someone keeps a dark secret. Who? What? Why?
The main character did something bad in the past. What was it? How does she feel about it? In what way does this past deed and remorse influence her actions now?
Is there another side to this?
Why does this disturb me so?
What does this situation remind me of?
What would this character need to be safe?

THE FREEWRITING EXPERIENCE

Many writers find that when they freewrite, after a while a story takes shape. You may find that, too, but don't be surprised if you need to chop off the first few pages.

More often, you get some exciting threads, but not a real story, or you get a story, but one that's so awful, it's not worth developing. No problem. Put it aside for an hour, a day or a month. Then re-read what you've written, and underline anything that piques your interest. You may find your heart beating faster, or your mind whispering "whoa!" during certain passages. Underline those.

Then start again, this time exploring one of the underlined angles in more depth.

Writing by the seat of your pants can be nerve-wracking when you're new to it. It's like driving somewhere without knowing the destination. But it can also be exhilarating. I find it works especially well with dark stories.

With several of my yarns, I wrote without having an idea where they would lead. For example with 'The Devil You Know' (which at the time had the working title 'No More Trains Tonight'), I had a character alone on a railway station platform in the middle of nowhere at night. It was a creepy yarn, but I had no idea where it would go. I knew something dangerous was going to happen – but what? A ruthless railway inspector? A hungry vampire? A pack of wolves? A panther escaped from the zoo?

I tried out several possibilities, and none of them worked. I almost despaired.

Then another idea came, and although it didn't feel special at the time, I tried it out. Suddenly, everything fell into place in a dark, chilling way. When I look at this story now, I can scarcely believe that I hadn't always known how it was meant to end.

If you like, you can read the story. I'm adding it to the back of this book.

ASSIGNMENT

Get a glass of water or a cup of tea, sit down comfortably, and set a kitchen timer or alarm clock to go off in one hour. Now write, and don't stop until the alarm rings.

CHAPTER 4: FIFTEEN MASTER PLOTS

This approach is different from the one in Chapter 3, but also leads to great stories. Try both methods and see which of them suits you best. I like to use both.

PLOT IDEAS YOU CAN USE

Certain fascinating storylines recur again and again in horror fiction, each time with a different slant. When you boil the stories down to basic plot skeletons and then flesh them out with your own imagination, you get fresh tales. Even if dozens of authors use the same basic plot, each writer's interpretation is different.

I've collected several plot templates for you to use. Which of these resonate with you? Which might be a good fit for the titles in your list? Which would work for the vague story idea that's been haunting you? Change or combine them as you like. Infuse them with your personal fears, populate them with individual characters, place them in unusual settings, and write them in your author voice.

The initialism 'MC' means 'the main character' or hero of your story.

1. MC hears about a danger (haunted room, ancient religion), mocks it as superstition, and sets out to prove it's not real. He enlists the help of a loyal but reluctant friend/servant/colleague/lover. In the supposed danger zone, he finds what he believes is evidence that he is right. But then things get stranger and stranger, and he and his friend find themselves in real danger. MC fights against the threat, narrowly getting away with his life. He and his friend relax for a moment

– and find that the danger is even worse than they had supposed. After a terrible ordeal, MC finally defeats the threat. He has escaped, but will never mock superstition again. His friend, however, has paid a terrible price – he is dead, crippled or insane.

2. A danger (mythical monster, evil human) threatens the community. MC is the only one who can defeat it. Her first try ends in failure. Her second try fails as well. Then she learns something important, grows as a character, and changes tactics drastically. She tries again, and this time she wins.

3. MC wants to belong to a community (an exclusive club, an inner-city gang, the in-crowd in the local pub, the popular girls in school, a secret society, an erotic scene, a religious cult, keepers of a secret). At first, it's mostly curiosity, but then he gets a taste of it and wants more. He works hard to convince members that he is worthy. He is granted basic initiation and a second experience that's so thrilling that he is completely hooked. He will do what it takes to get accepted to the inner circle and enjoy the pleasures to the full. When he's finally taken to the inner circle and involved in his third experience, he realises it is evil. What he thought of as desirable pleasure or a noble cause is a horrific exploitation of victims. But at this stage it is too late to back out (he has committed crimes, or witnessed so much that the gang can't let him live). Will he go ahead? Or will he back out and pay the price? This story has three possible endings, each terrible in its own way:
a) You can end the story with his realisation, leaving it open what he will do.
b) His conscience wins. Rather than aid evil, he sacrifices himself.
c) He decides to go ahead and enjoy the thrills as a full member of the group.

4. MC devotes herself to fighting evil. She brings great personal sacrifices (kills her friend, denounces her brother, breaks up with her fiancé) for the greater good. At last, she triumphs. Then she realises that what she thought was good was really evil, and that the supposed evil she fought was really good. Her friend, brother and fiancé were right, and she had been blinded by fanaticism.

5. An innocent (outsider, child) observes the actions and conversations of other people. On the surface, it seems harmless. But the reader picks up the subtext and knows there's something evil going on that the innocent doesn't understand.

6. MC is urged by spouse/colleague/friend not to pursue a dangerous venture. The annoyed MC does it anyway, to prove he's braver than the spouse/colleague/team mate thought. The venture is far more dangerous than he had thought. Confronting the danger, he nearly dies when his equipment fails, but escapes. If only he can reach/contact his spouse/colleague/friend/team mate/the helpline/the escape route he'll be safe. But she's not at the arranged meeting place/hasn't provided the support she promised. Worse, she has destroyed the shelter/disabled the helpline/blocked the escape route. MC realises the spouse/colleague/friend wants him to die, has set him up, needled him into the venture and prepared the trap. Bereft of support and illusions, he fights against the menace, and wins. The traitor falls into the trap she laid for the MC. The MC couldn't save her even if he wanted, because she has destroyed the means of rescue.

7. Newly dead MC wakes in a coffin, and rises as a ghost/zombie/vampire. She has unfinished business to conclude (wreaking vengeance, begging forgiveness, mending a wrong she has done) and will do what it takes to complete this task.

While adjusting to being undead in the world of the living, she experiences unexpected obstacles. She learns/understands/realises something she hadn't been aware of about herself/her spouse/her murderer/her death/her own guilt/her current state that leads her to question her mission. When she finally gets the chance to carry out her plan, she changes her mind and desists. She returns to her coffin and chooses permanent death.

8. MC is obsessed with hunting the serial killer/dragon/monster/evil creature. He doesn't listen to the pleas of his lover/spouse/child who wants him to stop. In the pursuit, he nearly dies, but prevails. He takes a trophy and looks forward to basking in the honour and glory. But first, he just wants to go home, spend time with his lover/spouse/child and make it up to them for his previous neglect. When he arrives home, he finds the killer/monster has ravaged his family. While searching for the monster, he had left his family unprotected, and they fell prey. The trophy in his hands has become meaningless.

9. MC believes that a supposedly dangerous/evil animal/person/creature/object is harmless and innocent. She sets out to win its trust/tame it/ protect it/train it/save it against the objections from family/spouse/neighbours. She devotes all her spare time and resources to taming/saving/training the animal/person/creature/object, and at the same time has to fight people's prejudices against the animal/person/creature/object who think it is dangerous/evil. She succeeds at last. While enjoying her triumph, she lets her guard down... and discovers too late that the animal/person/creature/object is dangerous/evil after all.

10. MC wants to overcome a personal weakness/prejudice/habit/fear. He fights against his habits and

instincts, and fails. He tries again, fails again. He tries once more, making a heroic effort, and succeeds. Now he discovers that in this instance he should have listened to his instincts after all. Too late - he has become an easy victim.

11. MC is nervous/apprehensive about a person/animal/object. She takes drastic precautions against it, but never feels really safe. At last, she acknowledges that her fears are irrational. The person/animal/object is harmless, and it was her unhealthy imagination that led her into this obsession. She dismantles her defences. Now the person/animal/object attacks.

12. MC is a semi-sympathetic character whom the reader can understand, but not quite like. He feels wronged by someone and obsessively plots to get the reward/justice/love he considers is his by right. He observes signs of danger but shrugs them off. When he gets worried, it's too late. He realises he has fallen into his own trap/walked into a rival's similar trap. Desperately, he tries to get out. He calls/begs/appeals to the very person whose downfall he had plotted. The situation gets worse, and the person ignores/mocks him. The story ends with MC in despair/terror realising he has brought about his own downfall.

13. MC is a righteous character who demands the highest moral standards of herself and others. She tolerates neither sin nor lax ethics, and obsessively demands that others do the right thing at all times. She lands in a situation where she has only two options. Both are immoral or ethically wrong and she must jettison one dearly held value in order to adhere to the other.

14. MC plots to bring about the downfall of another character. He is so focused on this that he neglects to see the bigger picture of what is going on. Then he realises that his supposedly loyal henchman has schemed to bring him down.

15. MC schemes to trap another person, priding herself in her ingenuity. She realises too late that the opponent has laid a trap for her. With her scheming, she has walked straight into the trap.

There are many other plots, so don't feel limited to the ones I've listed here. Use them as a starting point, and if they suit you, adapt them and make them your own. Just don't become so comfortable with one of the templates that you write story after story in the same pattern and nothing else, because this can lead to formulaic writing.

Many of my published stories use one of these plots, but in such altered ways that you won't recognise them unless you pay close attention to the structure.

CHAPTER 5: DARK FICTION AND HORROR GENRES

Your dark story can belong to more than one genre (and subgenre and subsubgenre). Here is a list to help you label your story, but please don't get hung up on definitions, because genres overlap, are part of other genres, and evolve constantly.

Your dark story might fight into these genres, even though not all fiction in all these genres is dark.

HORROR
This is the fiction of fear. It comes in many different forms and flavours, but it always seeks to rouse one or several facets of fear in the reader: apprehension, unease, revulsion, tension, horror, dread, panic, suspense or terror.

SPLATTERPUNK
This type of horror relies on extreme violence and graphic gore. There may be detailed descriptions of dismemberments, chainsaw massacres and disembowellings. Splatterpunk aims to shock, revolt and terrify. It seeks to create an immediate intense experience, rather than a lasting impression.

EXTREME HORROR
These stories seek to create the utmost terror in the reader. They turn up the horror to the highest possible volume, until the reader can't bear any more, and then they turn it up higher still. They are usually violent and often contain graphic descriptions of gory scenes. Extreme Horror and Splatterpunk overlap to a large extent.

PSYCHOLOGICAL HORROR
In this type of story, the danger comes from the human mind. It often explores questions of sanity, guilt, the nature of evil, the

justification of violence, the boundaries between right and wrong. In many psychological horror stories, the protagonist is the one who commits the atrocity. This look into the evil person's mind can be disturbing for the reader, and it may leave a lasting impression. Psychological Horror contains little or no violence and gore. Edgar Allan Poe's stories are masterpieces of Psychological Horror.

DYSTOPIAN
Dystopian fiction is set in a stark, nightmarish kind of world, often in the near future. As humans fight for survival and cling to their precarious existence, compassion, kindness and loyalty have become almost non-existent. The plot often revolves around someone giving love or loyalty and in return getting betrayed.

LOVECRAFTIAN
This genre is named after the author, H.P. Lovecraft, whose fiction inspired it. These stories are based on the concept that our world was once ruled by alien creatures, and that these monsters still exist out of sight, usually in the bowels of the earth, waiting to take over the world again. Some stories are spin-offs of Lovecraft's Cthulhu Mythos, others use original worlds with similar elements. Lovecraftian fiction straddles the fantasy and horror genres. It often features ancient secrets, slimy substances and main characters who are scholarly loners. It does not have much gore.

THRILLER
In this genre, suspense and anticipation are high. The story typically focuses on a highly intelligent, manipulative villain and the terrible deed he is about to commit against a helpless victim. Often, the villain is a serial killer preying on specific victim types. Victims and villains are human rather than supernatural.

Thrillers have strong elements of psychological horror and may contain graphic violence.

MYSTERY

These are crime stories which ask the question 'Whodunit?' or sometimes 'Howdunit?' or 'Whydunit?' They contain little or no violence and gore, but they may have elements of Psychological Horror, and they lend themselves to probing the boundaries between good and evil in the style of Dark Fiction.

DARK FICTION

The main meaning of this term is fiction that disturbs the reader by probing the boundaries between good and evil. In this sense, it often overlaps with Psychological Horror. Another meaning is Paranormal with dark or disturbing elements. The term can also be used as a pseudonym for Horror fiction, especially when talking to people who disdain Horror as crude and gross. The word 'dark' added to any other genre, e.g. 'Dark Science Fiction' or 'Dark Romance' suggests that the story has scary or disturbing elements.

SUPERNATURAL

Supernatural fiction is about people who face manifestations outside the normal human experience, such as hauntings, demonic possession, mind control. The mood is eerie, creepy, scary.
It is a subgenre of Fantasy and often includes elements of Horror, especially Psychological Horror.

PARANORMAL

This genre overlaps largely with Supernatural, but it usually features characters who are 'almost human' or 'formerly human' such as vampires, werewolves and zombies.

PARANORMAL ROMANCE

Stories in this genre typically feature a love relationship between a human and a paranormal person, such as a vampire or werewolf. It may have scary elements, and it may probe the boundaries between good and evil.

DARK FANTASY

This kind of story contains fantasy elements – often paranormal creatures or supernatural happenings – combined with scary or disturbing elements. Most Dark Fantasy straddles the Fantasy and Horror Genres.

URBAN FANTASY

Typically set in a run-down part of a modern city, these stories often feature human characters with magical or psychic abilities, as well as human-like characters such as zombies, werewolves and vampires. Urban Fantasy usually has both dark and scary elements, and often overlaps with Paranormal Romance and Thriller.

GOTHIC

This is an old fiction genre, dating back to the 18th and 19th century, and is the forerunner of most modern Horror fiction. It involves mysteries, dangerous secrets, melodrama, abuse of religious powers, fallen aristocracies, moral decay, bigamy, madness, hereditary curses, gloomy old buildings, death, ghosts, helpless innocent young victims and forbidden loves. As a literary genre, Gothic is experiencing a revival.

EROTIC HORROR

This type of fiction seeks to create two kinds of arousal in the reader – eroticism and fear. The plot is often based on lust driving characters to overstep moral boundaries and take risks they would not normally take. Erotic Horror can be

Psychological Horror, or it can be Splatterpunk – or anything in between.

HORROR COMEDY
Also called 'Humorous Horror', this genre combines Horror and comedy. Fear and laughter form a natural partnership. Often, it contains an element of parody, poking fun at popular films, books, situations or events.

ROMANTIC SUSPENSE
This genre evolved from Gothic and into Paranormal Romance, and overlaps with both. Stories may have Thriller, Horror, Supernatural and Paranormal elements as well. Typically, it features a female character in jeopardy who doesn't know whom she can trust. The setting plays a big role. It is often rural, isolated and creepy. The story contains no violence or gore.

STEAMPUNK
This is a curious blend of several genres, usually Science Fiction, Fantasy and Historical, and often – but not always - Horror. Other genres – such as Western, Erotica or Romance – may be added to the mix. The world-building is based on the idea that steam technology developed further than it did in reality. It often features mad scientists, obsessed inventors, monsters, ghosts, vampires, governesses, ladies and gentlemen, laboratories, clockwork mechanisms, airships, fog and corsets. The setting is usually urban and inspired by the 19th or early 20th century. Steampunk lends itself to scary scenes and also to an exploration of good and evil, especially regarding moral attitudes, class differences, racism, greed and abuse of power.

GHOST STORIES
Ghost stories can be found in most cultures and most periods. They belong to the Supernatural genre, and often also to Horror,

Psychological Horror, Gothic, Steampunk, Horror Comedy or Slipstream. They show the interaction between a supernatural entity and a living human. The mood is often creepy, but there is little violence and no gore.

SLIPSTREAM

These stories push the boundaries between mainstream fiction and fantasy fiction. The blend of real and fantastic gives the reader a surreal experience.

SPECULATIVE FICTION

This is a broad term encompassing the Fantasy and Science Fiction genres, as well as Horror Fiction with Supernatural or Paranormal elements. The stories are based on the world being not quite as we know it. It is a useful term when your story doesn't fit into any specific pigeon-holes.

WEIRD FICTION

This is an old term for Speculative Fiction, used in the early 20th century. Some writers are reclaiming it with pride.

FLASH FICTION

This is a modern term for very short stories. It's about the length rather than the content. Flash Fiction has a word count of no more than a thousand words, and is often even shorter. Because of its brevity, it doesn't allow much world-building or character development, but it lends itself to Slice Of Life stories, and flash-length Horror Comedy is popular. Often, Flash Fiction has only a single scene and ends with a twist.

SLICE OF LIFE

These stories have no obvious plot, but show a snapshot from people's ordinary lives. This format can work well for Psychological Horror and Dark Fiction.

CROSS-GENRE
When a story straddles two or more genres – such as Historical Horror or Science Fiction Horror Romance – this is referred to as Cross-genre. Cross-genre fiction used to be difficult to sell but is currently popular.

COLLECTION
A book containing several short stories – usually of the same genre or about the same theme, is a Collection.

ANTHOLOGY
When a book combines stories by several authors – usually of the same genre or about the same theme – it's an Anthology. Anthologies are Collections, but not all Collections are Anthologies.

Don't worry if your story doesn't match any of the descriptions precisely. Genres are far more flexible these days than they used to be. Just pick one or several genres which mostly fit.

Attempts to create a definite taxonomy of genres are futile. People can argue for hours over whether genre A is part of genre B or the other way round. If someone insists that all stories about zombies are Dystopian, that Romantic Suspense is always a subgenre of Gothic, or that Paranormal Romance can never be Horror, just smile sweetly and move on.

Use the labels when they're helpful, and ignore them when they're not.

When pitching to an agent or editor, they serve as shorthand to establish what kind of book it is. At pitchfests where you may have only three minutes to present your book, saying 'Dystopian

Horror Romance' or 'Science Fiction Splatterpunk' saves time.

If you submit to traditional publishers, mention the genre(s) in the query letter. When indie publishing (self-publishing), mention the genres in the back cover blurb, the catalogue and website description, and select suitable categories on Amazon.

If a publisher's 'Guidelines for Contributors' says they're currently open to short story submissions for a Dark Steampunk Anthology, you need to know whether the story you've just written would be a fit.

When chatting with writers, the genre labels make it easy to talk shop. You may tell me that you've started a Splatterpunk story, I share that my latest work in progress is Psychological Horror, and then we discuss the best way to introduce Gothic themes into our writing.

ASSIGNMENT

1. Consider the story you're writing or planning to write. Which of the categories would be a good fit?

2. Which of the categories appeal to you? You may want to consider these for future stories.

CHAPTER 6: POINT OF VIEW

For great intensity, write your story from the perspective of one single person, what she sees, hears, thinks, feels. This technique is called 'Deep Point of View', 'Limited Point of View', or simply 'Point of View' (PoV for short).

DEEP POV TECHNIQUES

Deep PoV is like real life: we know only one person's perspective. This gives deep PoV a strong sense of realism and creates an intense experience for the reader. The reader may become so absorbed that she forgets it's only a story. When this happens, you have succeeded as a writer.

For most dark stories, Deep PoV is the best choice.

Of course, Deep PoV has drawbacks, but there are ways around them.

* You can only show what the PoV character can see, not the important events that happen at the same time in a different place. For those, you may have to use devices such as phone calls, television news or telepathy.

* You cannot show what the PoV character looks like, unless you use tricks such a look in the mirror or a friend commenting on her looks.

* To convey what other characters think or feel, you depend on dialogue and body language.

* When the PoV character dies, the story is over, unless she turns into a vampire, ghost or zombie.

You can write Deep PoV in first person *(I did this)* or third person *(He/she did this)* Second person *(You did this)* is also possible, although this works for very few stories.

Which character should you choose for the PoV? This is normally the MC (main character), although you can also use a minor character. Ideally, the PoV is someone who is present throughout the story, and who has a lot at stake. Dark stories allow more creative uses than most other genres, so feel free to experiment. For example, you can write from the PoV of the evil villain or the greedy henchman. Even the PoV of a ghost, a piece of furniture or the devil himself are possible.

Delve as deeply into the PoV character's experience as possible, so the reader mentally becomes this person.

Here are some handy tricks:

* Don't say that the character saw/heard/thought/felt something. Just describe the experience. For example, instead of *'She heard the clock tick'* write *'The clock ticked'*. Instead of *'She wondered where John was'*, write *'Where was John?'*

* Show how the weather and the temperature affect the PoV character. Use physical descriptions. For example:
The ice-laden wind slipped through his cloak like needles of steel.
The chill numbed her fingers, then crawled further into every fibre of her body.
The heat of the pavement slabs burnt through the soles of my sandals.
The hot air seared his throat.

* Show how emotion affects the PoV character's body – especially fear in all its forms (such as anxiety, apprehension, terror and panic).

For example:

Her throat tightened with apprehension.
Dread pressed down on my chest.
Icy sweat trickled down her spine.
Cold fear crawled into his flesh.
Fear slithered through her insides.
Terror squeezed the air from his lungs.
Her knees quaked.
Terror welled up in a sickening wave.

SERIAL POINT OF VIEW

It's possible to use more than one character's PoV, one after the other. This is called 'Serial Deep PoV' or 'Multiple Limited PoV'. This can be useful in longer works of fiction such as novellas and novels.

Short stories use it less often, but it can work if your story is long, if the plot needs several perspectives, or if the story continues after the main character dies.

Serial Deep PoV doesn't give the same intense experience as Single Deep PoV, but the increased plot flexibility may be worth it. Avoid head-hopping (switching PoV often and suddenly). Instead, wait until there's a natural break in the story, such as the end of a scene. As soon as you've switched PoV, make it clear who the new PoV is, or the reader will be confused.

OMNISCIENT POINT OF VIEW

This is the god-like perspective, looking into everyone's heart and soul, seeing everything that goes on in the world, even in the future.

Omniscient PoV follows one character for a few paragraphs, then another, and in between it makes statements about the whole world. It may even deliver historical information or the author's moralising messages.

Here are some sentences that fit only into Omniscient PoV:
Lady Amelia thought all was lost, but unbeknown to her, rescue was already on the way.
All over the world, the undead were rising at the same time.
Penicillin could have saved Sir Ethelbert, but it was not discovered yet.
Of course, sinners always get punished in the end, and this case was no exception, as readers are going to find out soon.

It was popular with readers in the Victorian age who loved moralising messages. Most modern readers prefer the intense of experience of Deep PoV. However, for some stories, Omniscient PoV is perfect.

To make Omniscient PoV work, stay in each character's perspective for a short time, avoid head-hopping in mid-paragraph, and insert at least one PoV-neutral sentence before you enter the next character's head.

OTHER POINT OF VIEW STYLES

Of the rarer forms of PoV, three are worth considering:

* Cinematic PoV. This is like a video camera, not a person. It sees everything – but only from the outside, not inside anyone's head or heart, and it doesn't judge or evaluate. This allows great

plot flexibility, but may not bring great intensity or emotional involvement.

* Fly-on-the-Wall PoV. Here, the PoV is a person, but somehow is not involved in the action and has no stake in the outcome. It is rare, but can be useful for horror stories, for example when an unemotional witness reports how a massacre unfolded.

* Detached PoV. This is dry, factual reporting in an objective (or pseudo-objective) style, such as a newspaper article, bulletin or official report. Horrific events reported in this unemotional manner can be chilling to read.

ASSIGNMENT

Decide what's the best PoV for your story. If in doubt, choose Deep PoV. Whose story is it? Can you tell all the crucial events from this person's perspective? What feels more natural – first or third person?

CHAPTER 7: MANAGING TENSION

A dark story needs tension and suspense, probably more than most other stories do. Over the two following chapters, I'll share my favourite techniques for achieving both.

What's the difference between 'tension' and 'suspense'?

Here's a simple explanation: Tension makes the reader care, while suspense makes the reader want to read on. Tension relates mostly to relationships between characters and the situation in which the main character is right now because of what happened before. Suspense is mostly about what will happen next.

The meanings overlap, and the words are often used interchangeably, so don't get stuck up on the definitions. What matters is that both make your story exciting and keep your readers riveted.

GOAL

The quickest way to make the reader root for your MC is to give that character a goal, something she needs to achieve. This may be the same goal throughout the story, or it can change as the situation changes.

For example, in the first scene the goal may be *Bill needed to prove that the mansion was not haunted*, and in the second *Bill needed to get out of the mansion before the ghosts killed him*.

The words *want, need, have to* or *must* are useful in this sentence.

If you're writing deep PoV, you can simply state the goal:

Bill had to...
Mary needed to...
She wanted to...
He must find a way to...

You can also put it in dialogue:
"I'll kill the monster or die trying."
"I have to get past the guards somehow."

You may want to state the goal more than once, perhaps every few paragraphs, each time phrased differently.

RAISING THE STAKES

Emphasise why the MC needs to achieve this goal. Give her an important reason, or better still, several reasons.

What would be the dire consequences of failure?

If a young woman doesn't get out of the cave, the monster will devour her alive. That's strong. But you can make it stronger: if she doesn't get out of the cave, the monster will devour her and her baby.

A teenage boy must prove his courage by leaping across an abyss in order to be accepted as a gang member. That's strong. Raise the stakes: if he doesn't pass this test, no other gang will give him a chance.

The more you put at stake, the greater the tension, the more the reader cares.

CONFLICTS AMONG CHARACTERS

Create tension by giving the characters in your story conflicting goals. If character A achieves his goal, character B can't achieve hers. Even if they both want the same thing – to kill the monster, to free the prisoner – they may have different opinions on how to achieve this, they may clash over who is the leader in the venture, or old unresolved issues between them bubble to the surface. Contrasting moral values and ethical standards can also lead to conflict.

The characters don't have to fight or even argue. Sulking silence or simmering resentment can add a layer of tension.

Avoid characters who are in agreement over all important matters.

PEAKS AND TROUGHS

If you keep the tension continuously high, the effect wears off. Instead of being roused further, the readers become bored.

To prevent this, slacken the tension from time to time... and then tighten it further.

Imagine the waves on a stormy sea. The peaks are only high because of the troughs between them. If there were only continuous peaks without any troughs, the sea would be flat.

You need to create the troughs which make the peaks look high. This allows the reader to relax, but only for a moment, because as soon as her heart has slowed a little, you increase the tension even more.

In a scary story, you do this by moving your character to a position of relative safety where she can catch her breath, bandage her wounds, and reflect on her situation. In a psychological story, you can bring about a temporary conciliation or seeming solution.

Insert a trough between the two most frightening sections of your story, or between the scenes of greatest interpersonal conflict. If you have a scene where the terror goes on for longer than the reader can bear, break it up by inserting a short trough before the reader becomes immune.

One trough may suffice for your story, though you may use several. A trough doesn't need to be long. A couple of paragraphs is often enough, because you don't want your reader to become too relaxed.

You can see an example of this technique in my story 'Seagulls' which I've included at the end of this book. The paragraphs where Josie takes a lavender-scented bath and shaves her legs serve no other purpose but to create a trough between peaks of tension.

ASSIGNMENT

1. Decide what your MC wants or needs to achieve in several places in your story.

2. Find a way to raise the stakes. What additional reasons would make it even more important that the MC achieves her goal?

3. What kind of conflict could exist between the characters? How do their goals, plans or values clash? Who envies/resents/mistrusts whom?

4. Identify a spot in your story where a trough would serve to

heighten the peaks. Write that trough.

CHAPTER 8: BUILDING SUSPENSE

Suspense and tension overlap, so to increase the suspense, you can also use the techniques discussed in the previous chapter.

POSE A QUESTION

Plant a question in the reader's mind, something for which she wants to find an answer. This will drive her to read on.
What is going to happen? This is the best question, because it suits almost every scene in every story, and it keeps the reader on the edge of her seat.
What has happened? This question can work well for the Mystery genre, and also for short sections in other stories.
What is happening? This is a great question for Horror stories, but don't overdo it. Mystify the PoV and the reader for a few paragraphs, but not more. Otherwise the reader thinks *What the heck is going on? This doesn't make sense, I don't understand what's going on, there's no point reading more.*
Remember my advice in the previous chapter, about giving the MC a goal? Create a question around this goal: *Will the MC achieve the goal?* Or perhaps: *How will the MC achieve the goal?*

THE TICKING CLOCK

Give your protagonist a time limit by when she must have achieved her goal or reached safety. Perhaps she must get out of the castle before dusk when the vampires stir to life. Or she has to disable the bomb which is set to explode in precisely ten minutes.

Then put obstacles in her way to make this almost impossible. Show frequently how the time passes: the sun sinks towards the horizon, the minute hand of the watch moves.

This technique is often used in the Thriller genre and can create almost unbearable suspense.

PACING

Vary the pace according to the content of the scene. When the action is fast – races, fights – use fast-pace techniques with short sentences, few thoughts, no descriptions.

However, when the suspense is great, you can increase it even more by slowing the pace. When the reader sits on the edge of her seat, biting her nails, desperately needing to find out what happens next, keep her waiting.

This technique works especially well when the MC is unable to do anything. Perhaps she is tied to the chair, and the murderer approaches with a knife. Or maybe she is handcuffed in a cell, knowing that in precisely twelve minutes the building will blow up.

To slow the pace in such situations, insert sentences of description. My favourite method is describing irrelevant background noises. They can drive the reader crazy with excruciating suspense.

Examples:
Upstairs, a toilet flushed, and water gurgled through the pipe in the wall.
Somewhere outside, a seagull screeched.
The guard's boots clanked rhythmically down the corridor.
Rodent feet scurried.

THE DOOR OPENS

Here's a nifty trick for increasing suspense: Put a door between the MC and the danger. This creates a psychological barrier, her last chance to turn back.

Any kind of 'door' can serve: a front door, an entry arch, a trap door, garden gate, a stile, a cave mouth. Slow the pace by describing the door and how it opens. As always, sounds are effective.

The door's white paint was flaking, revealing previous coats of scarlet and black.
The knobs of the three doorbells were sticky with grime.
'Strictly No Entry. Danger Zone', the sign on the door warned.
The double door had cracked glass panels and chipped brown paint, plastered with notices for last year's events.
While she waited, steps shuffled inside, and then a key scraped in the lock.
The door swished open.
The door opened with a squeal.
The door whined inwards on its hinges.
The door rattled open.

ASSIGNMENT

1. Choose a question to create in your reader's mind for at least part of the story. Find a way to express this question. You may be able to simply spell it out.

2. Would a Ticking Clock effect work for your story? If yes, what must MC achieve, by when? Decide how to show the passing of time, and write at least two sentences about this to insert in different places.

3. What's the most suspenseful moment of your story? Consider slowing the pace. Write a sentence about a background noise.

4. Does MC pass through a door on the way to danger? If not, consider inserting such a moment. Write a sentence describing what the door looks like, and another one describing how the door opens.

CHAPTER 9: HOW TO SCARE YOUR READERS

In this chapter, I'll share my favourite tricks for giving readers a good fright. You can combine them with the techniques I've presented in the previous chapter, because suspense enhances fear.

DARKNESS

For humans, everything is more frightening when they can't see much in the dark. Can your scene take place at night, or in a windowless room? Perhaps a power-cut has shut down the electric lighting. Maybe a gust of wind blows out the candle flame, or a bullet shatters the single light-bulb.

If absolute darkness doesn't fit into the story, aim for semi-darkness: dusk, a single lantern at night, a heavily curtained window, a thick canopy of trees blocking the sun. Flickering lights and shadows can create creepy effects.

To make the scene even creepier, let the darkness increase gradually: Perhaps night falls, or the camp-fire subsides, or the candles burn down one by one, or thickening clouds block the light of the moon.

Here are some examples of how you can describe full or partial darkness:
The sun set, leaving a red-gashing wound between the earth and the sky.
Darkness came down like a hood.
The darkness wrapped tightly around them.
The light of the lantern shuddered in the darkness.
The candle sputtered. The light wavered.
The lamp cast its smoky light on the brick walls.

The night was silent, but for the dry rustling of leaves as the wind whispered through the trees.

In the dark, humans can see little or nothing, and the other senses take over. Describe what the PoV smells, hears and touches.

SOUND

Of all the senses, the sense of hearing serves best to create excitement and fear. To make your scene scarier, simply insert several sounds into your draft.

Here are some ideas: the clacking of the villain's boots on the floor tiles, the ticking of the wall clock, a dog barking outside, the roaring of a distant motor, a door slamming somewhere in the house, water dripping from the ceiling, the chair squeaking, the whine of the dentist's drill, the scraping of the knife on whetstone, a faraway siren wailing, the heroine's own heartbeat thudding in her ears.

The sounds don't have to be part of the plot. They can be unconnected background noises. When the suspense is high, the description of an unconnected background noise can raise the suspense even higher.

The mention of sounds works especially well in combination with darkness, because the human sense of hearing is sharpened in the dark. Without light, your heroine becomes aware of many sounds she would not otherwise notice.

CHILL

If the temperature drops, the fear factor rises. Make it uncomfortably cold for the MC, and the readers will shiver with him. This works well in combination with darkness, because dark places are often cold. The power-cut which switched off the lights stops the heating, too. Nightfall brings colder temperature at the same time as darkness.

Other ideas: perhaps it's winter, or evening, or perhaps a cool breeze chills everything. Maybe the owner of the place has turned the heating off to save energy, or maybe the survivors have run out of fuel, or perhaps the ceiling fan is over-active. Stone buildings, caves, and subterranean chambers tend to be cold.

Describe how the cold feels to the protagonist, how her skin pimples, how she rubs her arms to get warm, how her fingertips turn blue, how she shivers.

To turn up the suspense further, consider dropping the temperature lower and lower as the weather gets worse, as the fuel gets sparser, or as the heroine crawls deeper into the old mine shaft. This creates an even stronger effect than if it's cold throughout.

The opposite can also be effective: Turn up the temperature to make the MC sweat. Perhaps there's an over-active stove, an overheated motor, or sweltering summer heat.

ISOLATION

Let the events unfold in an isolated location where few people ever go: an abandoned factory, a remote mountaintop, the depth of an unexplored cave. This creates eerie atmosphere and means that nobody is around to save the MC from danger.

Let your MC face the threat alone. Even if he has friends,

supporters and allies at the beginning of the story, they refuse to join this crazy quest, quarrel, desert, or betray him to the villain.

To make matters even worse, destroy all means of communication. The mobile phone's battery is dead, the landlines have been cut, and screams don't penetrate the dungeon walls.

Nobody else even knows where the MC is, because he changed his plans at short notice and did not tell anyone, so no rescue can be expected.

MEET THE MONSTER

When describing the threat – whether that's a psychopath, a shark or a dragon – focus on detail. You can devote one or several sentences to each detail.

However, give only a few details at a time. If you show everything at once, you leave nothing to build up to, so spread them out.

Good details to show are:
* Hands, fingers, nails, talons, claws
* The sound of the voice, growl, roar
* The smile, the teeth
* The texture of the skin, fur, scales

For more ideas about this, see Chapter 14.

GET VISCERAL

If you want to scare your readers, never tell them that the MC is scared. Instead, describe the fright in a way that allows the reader to feel it.

Fear affects the body. Describe these physical effects.

Examples:
My skin crawled.
Her scalp prickled and her breath stalled.
Fear clenched like a tight first around his chest.
Tendrils of terror curled into my stomach.
Cold sweat trickled down her sides.
His heart thudded louder and louder.
Fear clogged her throat.
My pulse pounded in my ears.
Cold sweat glued the blouse to my back.
Chills chased up my spine.
A ball of terror formed in my stomach.
My stomach knotted.
A weight seemed to press on her chest, robbing her of breath.

These sentences work better than *'He felt afraid'* and *'She was extremely frightened'*.

THE GORY BITS

This advice applies mostly to Splatterpunk stories. If you want to shock your readers with violence and gore, make the descriptions graphic, but keep them short.

Instead of describing everything, focus on a couple of details – the brains spilling from the child's cracked skull, the eyeball hanging on the cheek, the intestines lying beside the body. Describe the colours, textures and smells.

However, don't go on for more than two or three sentences, or the effect will wear off. Non-stop gore doesn't shock; it bores. A better strategy is to describe one gory detail, then switch to something else for a few sentences before you zoom in on another bit of gore.

To clog the reader's throat with emotion, create a contrast between the gore and a peaceful, innocuous image. The child's mutilated corpse still clutches the doll. The brain from the baby's split skull spills across the fluffy pink blanket.

You can also use similes, comparing the gruesome bits to something from everyday life: The intestines look like spaghetti in tomato sauce. The blood spilling from the teenager's mouth looks like she's applied even more lipstick than usual. This can create a touch of black humour which diffuses the tension but at the same time increases the horror of the situation.

ASSIGNMENT

Choose three of these techniques – whichever suit your story best. Write one sentence for each of them.

CHAPTER 10: CREEPY LOCATIONS

Choosing the right setting is even more important for dark stories than for most other kinds of fiction.

Sometimes, a place can inspire a story. Look at the ideas you generated in the Chapter 1 assignment: did you list any creepy places? Freewrite about what's so creepy about one of these locations, or about what terrible thing might have happened there.

At other times, a place can make a story interesting, and elevate a good story to great. If you've written a story that's all right but not special, try rewriting it with a different setting. It may suddenly take off.

Most often, the place alone doesn't yield enough material for a story, but if you combine it with other items from your list, the mixture sizzles: that abandoned factory plus disturbing greed and your fear of enclosed spaces... that remote cemetery plus distressing deception plus your fear of being buried alive...that ruined temple plus religious fanaticism plus your fear of torture... The list yields endless possible combinations, and each of them can make a winning story.

My mind is like a revolving drum filled with hundreds of jigsaw pieces, each representing a story idea. Sometimes two or more pieces click together, and that's when a story takes shape. The location is almost always one of the first jigsaw pieces to click.

Many of my short stories are inspired by the places where I have lived and travelled. I live in a small dilapidated town of former Victorian grandeur on the south coast of England, and if you know the region, you may recognise the locations that inspired some of the tales. The landscapes around Lake Constance where I grew up also feed my imagination, as do my vibrant memories of Turkey, Tunisia, China and Nepal.

Sometimes years pass before I find the right plot for an eerie location. This happened with my story 'Scruples'. The ferocious force of wind and waves sometimes erodes the English cliffs and breaks off whole sections. The first time I walked below Fairlight Cliffs near Hastings, the sight made my throat constrict. A large chunk of the cliff had recently fallen, leaving houses half destroyed, half standing. From below, I could see the inside of living rooms and kitchens, still furnished, as if at any moment the inhabitants would enter. For years, the sight haunted me, but I could not come up with a story, although I made several starts. I also tried to write a story about the violent storms that battered the Sussex coast in 1287; these attempts also petered out. Then the two ideas clicked together – what if someone is trapped inside a medieval house that breaks apart in the storm? Now the tale took shape quickly as a historical Horror story.

SELECT THE SETTING

Here are some ideas for great settings:

* Anything that's on your list. Places which creep you out are perfect.

* Weird places. A dinosaur museum, a cowshed, a fun fair, a lighthouse, a pottery workshop, a diamond mine, a cruise ship, a children's petting zoo... Take your readers to places they don't visit every day.

* Supposedly safe places. A child's nursery, a family kitchen, a school playground, a classroom, a corner shop... place the horror in a location where your readers expect to be safe, and you can scare them witless.

* Isolated places. A rowing boat on a lake, the slope of a mountain in the Alps, a deserted farmhouse in the Yorkshire Moors... Cut off from all help and support, your character is helpless.

* Enclosed spaces. A cable car, a mine shaft, a helicopter, a stalactite cave... This can make the story scary, especially if the victim is trapped with the perpetrator. If you explore the dark aspects of people's relationships, the fact that nobody can walk away intensifies the conflicts. Enclosed spaces also help to keep the story short, because everything unfolds in a single scene.

INSPIRING PICTURES

Photos can provide visual inspiration. I have collected many photos of creepy and spooky places in a Pinterest Board, and I plan to write about these locations one day. You're welcome to visit, pick a photo, and let your imagination soar.

So far, the collection has 171 images, and I'm constantly adding new ones. They are mostly abandoned sites – mansions, factories, vehicles, amusement parks, theatres – and decaying buildings. Some of them give me shudders, others possess an eerie beauty.

http://www.pinterest.com/raynehallauthor/raynes-spooky-creepy-places-collection/

HOW TO DESCRIBE THE SETTING

Give your readers an intense experience of the place, as if they were really there. Use the senses to create atmosphere, especially if you want your story to be frightening or creepy.

Here are some ideas:

* Describe a small visual detail that is in itself harmless, but hints at secrets, danger or decay:
Weeds poked through the cracks in the broken paving-slabs.
The pavement was slippery with rain, pale stalks and rotten leaves.
The tiles were grime-streaked and flecked with mould.
Below the rich velvet curtain, the wallpaper peeled, exposing raw brick.
A fly lay on the windowsill, its legs curled in death.

* Mention several smells. Of all the senses, smell has the greatest effect on the reader's subconscious. A single sentence listing a smell is enough to transport the reader to that place:
The air smelled of nicotine and stale beer.
The room smelled of pizza and unwashed socks.
The fresh scents of salt and seaweed mingled with the odour of rotting fish.
The smell of bleach warred with the odours of vomit and piss.

* Sounds serve to increase the suspense and excitement. Use them liberally throughout the story.
A car door slammed, and a motor whined.
An owl hooted in the distance.
Ceiling fans whirred, cutlery clanked, and the espresso-maker hissed with steam.
Water roared down the ravine and splashed against the rocks.
The door squealed on its hinges.
The straw-stuffed mattress wheezed.

* The source and quality of light adds atmosphere. Insert a sentence showing where the light in the place comes from, and what it looks like.

The light bulb cast a pale glow in the centre of the room.
Two beams of white light pierced the darkness.
A sliver of sunlight peaked through the crack between the curtains.
Lightning flashed in sharp, blinding blinks
Golden sunlight poured through the window.
Houses gleamed white in the late afternoon sun.
Shafts of torchlight struggled through the viscous darkness.
Raindrops made needle streaks in the sulphurous light of the street lamps.

* Describe how the temperature affects the characters, especially the PoV. This is particularly effective if the temperature grows either hotter or colder.

Relentless chills gnawed through the thin layer of her jacket.
Gusts of icy wind drove sleet into my face.
She tried to rub warmth back into her stiff fingers.
Sweat trickled down the small of her back and into the cleft between her buttocks.
The broiling heat seared his lungs with every breath.

PRACTICAL RESEARCH

If you can, spend some time in the location of your choice – that abandoned factory, that eerie castle ruin – and take notes.

This is fun and exciting, although it may challenge your courage. I even spent a night in a remote cemetery once to research the atmosphere for a ghost story, observing every flickering shadow and listening to every creepy noise. I jotted down how the wooden gate creaked on unoiled hinges, how the gravel crunched under my steps, and how the twigs of the trees beckoned like skeleton fingers, withered and pale. As a result, the story 'Take Me To St. Roch's' is authentically creepy.

If the place exists only in your imagination, visit one that is similar. For example, if your story plays out in a medieval tavern, you could visit your local pub, and if the setting is a mountain on the other side of the globe, you could climb a peak closer to home.

It also pays to take notes for future stories. When you find yourself in a creepy, weird or interesting place – perhaps when you're travelling or holidaying abroad - collect descriptions. Don't rely on your memory, which will only store general impressions, but watch out for small details.

Whenever you have time to kill – in the dentist's waiting room, at the laundrette, during a long railway journey - get out your notebook and describe the place. One day you may write a dark comedy set in a laundrette, a ghostly tale about a haunted train, or a horror story about an evil dentist.

Always keep a notebook and pens on you. I recommend you also carry this worksheet with prompts. You may want to paste a copy of it into your notebook.

SETTING RESEARCH CHECKLIST

* What noises are there? Find at least five sounds, and describe them with verbs.
* What does this place smell of? Find at least two smells. This can be difficult, but is worth it.
* A small visual detail which most people would overlook, but which is somehow characteristic of the place.
* A signpost, notice, framed picture, announcement or sign.
* A description of the floor, ground or carpet.
* The source and quality of the light (where does the light come from? How bright is it, what colour?)
* Something which seems out of place.

* A person. How is s/he dressed? How does s/he move? Watch especially the posture, the facial expression and repeated movements.

* A simile, comparing something in this place to something outside the place. For example '... looks like...', '...sounds like...', '...smells like....', '... as big as...', '... as if....', '... slower than...', '...reminds me of...'

* A door. What does the door look like? How does it sound when it opens? How does it sound when it closes?

* Touch. How something feels when you touch it (e.g. Is the doorknob cold, warm, rough, smooth, sticky?)

ASSIGNMENT

1. Choose a location for your story.

2. Write a sentence about smells in this place and one about sounds.

3. Go to a place outside your home, and take notes – either for your current story or for something you may write in the future.

CHAPTER 11: MAKE THE MOST OF THE WEATHER

The weather is an easy way to enrich your story with realism and atmosphere. Here are some ways you can use it.

CREATE ATMOSPHERE

Describe noises, temperature changes, smells and visual details. This applies especially to outdoor scenes, but if the story takes place indoors, the weather outside still deserves a mention.

Examples:
Rain puckered the surface of the water.
The golden stone of the walls glowed in the autumn sunshine.
The lawn shimmered with frost.
Rain pattered softly in the trees above them.
The rain sharpened the smells of smoke and earth.
Wind rattled the shutters.
A smoky coal stove struggled to drive out the cold.
The wind rose, tugging at street banners, tossing plastic litter into the air, piling dead leaves against the walls.
Fat lethargic flakes drifted past the window.
The sun persisted, and water drops prattled from roofs and railings, from poles and porches.
The road glistened with black patches of molten tarmac.

DEEPEN THE POV

Write a sentence about how the weather affects the PoV. Focus on the physical experience. This will make the reader experience the situation and forget that it's a story.

Examples:
Her cardigan clung to her body, sodden and cold, and her boots

squelched with water.
Wind sang past my ears.
Icy wind pierced her knitted sweater.
Needles of hail pricked her face, as if she had dipped her head into a pincushion.
His cheeks stung from the hail's insistent pounding.
Relentless chills gnawed through the thick layers of his winter coat.
The chill numbed her fingers, then crawled further into every fibre of her body.
Sweat ran in streams from his forehead and dripped into his eyes.
Inside the train, air-conditioned cool enveloped me like a soothing caress.
The heat of the pavement slabs burnt through the soles of my sandals.
Sweat soaked into her shirt, her knickers, her bra.

MAKE IT DIFFICULT FOR THE CHARACTERS

Think of ways to use the weather to make things uncomfortable and difficult for the MC.
Maybe he faces a long trek through the broiling heat with neither water nor shade. Perhaps she flees from the monster, but slips on the icy pavement. Or he must not leave any tracks, but his feet sink into the mud with every step.

STRAINED TEMPERS

Weather affects how people feel and act. After weeks of grey skies and rain, the lack of sunlight makes some people lethargic and others grumpy. Heat can make people short-tempered and more aggressive than usual. Foul weather can make your characters so impatient to reach shelter that they neglect safety, lose patience with others, overlook danger signs, or make foolish mistakes.

MOOD AND FOREBODING

You can manipulate the reader's mood with weather descriptions. If you want the reader to feel what the PoV does, use words that convey that emotion.

Examples:
PoV is happy, cheerful, content or in love
The wind caressed the branches and sent golden leaves dancing.
Frost silvered the garden with diamond sparkles.
PoV is angry, frustrated or unhappy
Wind lashed the branches and ripped off the last leaves.
Frost smothered the garden with merciless chill.

If you like, you can use the weather description to place a subtle hint that something bad is about to happen, even though the PoV is still happy and unaware. For this technique, apply words that have negative or ominous connotations.

Examples:
The sky bruised into night.
Sodden leaves clogged the gutters.
The sun slammed hard shadows against the wall.

BEWARE THE PATHETIC FALLACY

Describing the weather filtered through the PoV's mood is good – but selecting the weather to reflect the mood can lead to clichéd writing.

If your PoV feels inner turmoil, don't automatically show roiling clouds. If the PoV is sad, this doesn't mean it has to rain, and a PoV in love doesn't call for instant sunshine.

The assumption that the weather changes to adapt to a character's mood is called Pathetic Fallacy. You can use it if you like, and if you're a novice writer, it can be useful practice. But once you've progressed beyond beginner level, you may want to leave the Pathetic Fallacy behind.

Your writing will be fresher if you contrast the weather with the PoV's mood. Describe what thunderclouds look like to a girl who is happily in love, or how golden sunshine annoys the grumpy guy.

COLLECTING DESCRIPTIONS

Keep a notebook with weather descriptions. Observe all kinds of weather throughout the year, and jot down detailed notes.

Then, when you need to describe a thunderstorm or a heat wave, you can look up those descriptions. They will be more vivid than anything you can imagine or dredge up from your memory.

ASSIGNMENT

1. Decide what the weather in your story is like. Write three sentences describing it. Include one sentence that hints at the PoV's mood, and one about how the weather affects the PoV physically.

2. Go outside or look out of the window. What's the weather like right now? Write some descriptive sentences for use in a future story.

CHAPTER 12: HOW TO OPEN YOUR STORY

Your first paragraph is the finger that beckons the reader. It promises: 'Come inside, and you'll find something worthwhile'.

Above all, it needs to convey the kind of story that's to come. From the beginning, the reader needs to know – or at least suspect – that they're in for a dark experience.

This can be difficult to achieve, especially with Horror fiction. If you open the story with a horror situation – acute danger, gory violence, extreme brutality – it's impossible to build up from there.

Avoid extremes. Instead, start quietly and let it escalate. 'Quiet' doesn't mean boring. Aim to introduce suspense, and perhaps other subtle flavours of fear: unease, foreboding.

How do you achieve this?

Here are my three favourite ways to open dark and scary stories. Try them out. One of them may fit your story.

OPENING WITH SETTING DESCRIPTION

Start by showing the place, focusing on the details that create a slightly creepy effect: light and shadow, temperature and noises.

Filter this through the PoV character's experience.

Here are examples from my own stories. You may find them inspiring, although your personal style will of course be different.

Prophetess
The noon sun slams hard shadows on the road, and my sandalled feet stir up yellow dust. At this time of the day, the walls of Troy afford no refuge from the violent heat. Where latticed balconies once granted sheltering shade, stark limestone glares and empty entrances gape like scurvy mouths, the wood plundered for cooking fires. The air is dry, as if moisture as well as wealth had been sucked out of the city, and soured with pangs of urine. The whole lower town stinks of suffering, of fear and decay.
Father has invited me to the midday meal, a gesture of reconciliation.

Only A Fool
The *clack-clack-clack* of your heels echoes through the night-empty street. The drizzle paints needle-streaks in the light of the fake Victorian lamps. Already, the pavement grows slippery with roadside rubbish, rain and rotten leaves. You should have called a taxi while you had the chance. Now it's too late. Around here, the payphones are vandalised.

Take Me To St. Roch's
Jean hated silence. It gnawed at her nerves and sapped her spirits, especially during night-time drives. Maybe she should give up teaching evening classes, and try to get by on her widow's pension alone. Or perhaps she should scrape together the money to buy a radio for her car.
In the darkness, the slopes of the Sussex Downs sank into valleys, and woodlands merged into fields. The windscreen wipers screeched across the glass, smearing dirt with the remnants of a November drizzle. At least the sound kept the silence out.

Double Rainbows
Gerard hurried down the spiral staircase of Sibyl's lighthouse, his

shoes clanking on the metal steps. The blue steel hands of his Rolex showed 8.13. The tide had turned two hours ago, and he did not want to get his new boots wet as he hiked home.
The steep chalk path from the promontory to the seabed was slippery with smudge from the night's rain. The sea surface glinted like a diamond-sprinkled sheet, and the air smelled of salty seaweed. In the distance, gulls cackled and squealed.

OPENING WITH DIALOGUE

Someone says something so startling, it grabs the readers' attention and rouses their curiosity.

Make it clear who is talking, otherwise the readers will be confused.

The most natural and engrossing way to start with dialogue is if the first speaker is not the point-of-view character. Instead, the PoV hears the words and replies or reacts.

Here are examples.

<u>Each Stone, A Life</u>
"Executions are so much pleasanter in the garden," Kirral said, leading the way up the steps into the pergola. "Birdsong, the scent of roses... From here, we have a perfect view. Take a seat."
He gestured to a pink divan beneath the rose-clad arch.
Leta sat, her legs tight together, palms on her thighs, and stared at her feet, resolved not to let the spectacle affect her.
Kirral sank into the cushions beside her and placed his hot be-ringed hand on hers. "My dear Lady Leta, you are trembling. Do you find the morning too chill?"

<u>Arete</u>

My husband blanches. "You've done - what?" His eyes are wide, his lips part, and he mops his brow with the sleeve of his immaculate chiton.

Greywalker
"You smell of death," the witch said. Her age-mottled nose wrinkled in disapproval.
"You speak truly, honoured one." Turgan bowed. "I am indeed dying."
Oil lamps flickered between rodent skulls, and somewhere in the back of the cave, water dripped.
Turgan kept his gaze lowered, as befitted a man addressing a crone. "A fungus devours my flesh. Already my blood is sour and my liver is cold, and the healer says I'll cross the life-end river before the new moon. I beg your forgiveness for my discourtesy in entering your home under this shadow, but I need your help."
The witch's eyes narrowed. "You think I will fight death for you? Go away, fool."
He shifted his weight. Already, his knees ached from standing. "I just need more time."

OPENING WHILE ALL SEEMS WELL WITH THE WORLD

This can be a powerful start for a disturbing story. Show characters in a peaceful situation – a family sharing dinner in the kitchen, a courting couple picnicking in a meadow, children paddling in an inflatable pool.

Introduce a small disquieting element early on, something not particularly worrying or dangerous, but enough to jar the perfection.

Examples:

Seagulls

While the stencils dried above the dado rail, Josie squatted on the carpet, eating her first breakfast in the new studio flat.

Three seagulls stood outside the window, white-feathered and silver-winged, their eyes yellow halos around death-dark cores. Every time Josie lifted a spoonful of muesli to her mouth, their greedy stares followed her hand.

Four Bony Hands

It was February, the time of Imbolc, and frost painted ice flowers on the window panes.

In the cosy warmth of her cottage in the clearing, Estelle munched freshly baked gingerbread and sipped hot cinnamon tea. She was spreading her tarot cards – The Knight of Wands: an unexpected visitor; the Five of Chalices: unseen danger – when she became aware of movements outside.

Burning

Supper was bangers and mash with mushy peas. Mum had promised me the glossy calendar photo for November - lambs frolicking around Camber Castle - but only if I ate up every meal this month. I disliked greasy bangers, I despised mash, and I hated mushy peas, but I wanted that picture, and it was only the ninth. Half-listening to my parents' grown-up talk about the need for a new church, I stirred the peas into the mash. Instead of becoming more appetizing, the meal now looked like a vomit puddle around dog turds.

ASSIGNMENT

Decide which type of opening suits your story best, and write the first 100 words.

CHAPTER 13: HOW TO END YOUR STORY

The ending needs to satisfy the reader – but it doesn't need to be a happy ending. With a dark story, the ending can be disturbing or gruesome.

Your story needs to end on a strong note. This is one of the challenges of the Horror genre. Once the reader has come face-to-face with the monster or been terrified out of her wits by a horrific situation, anything else is a let-down. Think carefully about the ending, and find ways to keep the tension high. Stirring the readers' emotions can be a good strategy.

ENDINGS TO AVOID

Novice writers tend to write stories with anticlimactic endings: The danger was merely imagined, the experience was only a training simulation or a computer game, the monster was a harmless pet, the stalker wasn't really evil but MC's long lost brother separated at birth... and worst of all: MC wakes up and it was all a dream.

SEVEN POSSIBLE ENDINGS

1. MC defeats the monster. Good triumphs over evil, and all is well. This is satisfying and gives the reader the relief she craves. It works especially well for children's stories. However, stories with this type of ending seldom leave a lasting impact.

2. MC defeats the monster, but wonders if the price was too high. This ending is similar to the first one, but it adds depth and leaves the readers with a lingering question. They will keep thinking about the story long after they've finished reading.

3. The monster defeats MC. In most genres, this would be unacceptable – but in short Horror fiction, the good guy may meet a gruesome death.

4. MC defeats the monster, but it was only a minor monster. The real monster is just stirring. This is a popular device in Horror fiction. It leaves the reader with a good scare.

5. MC defeats the monster – and realising that in doing so, he has unleashed greater evil. This is similar to the fourth, but deeper and darker.

6. MC defeats the monster – but regrets it. This type of ending is dark and leaves the reader thinking about right and wrong. Stories with this ending can have a powerful impact.

7. It's not clear what will happen. Open endings can leave the readers involved long after they've put the book down. However, they need to be handled with great skill, otherwise they leave the reader frustrated. A good finishing point is where MC has achieved the power to make a decision, leaving it open what she decides.

LEAVE QUESTIONS IN THE READER'S MIND

If you want the readers to remember your story, create an ending that leaves them wondering. Plant questions in the reader's mind. However, don't make them wonder, *What was that all about?* because that question leaves them frustrated. Instead, put them in the frame of mind where they probe their own conscience. *What would I have done in the hero's situation? Would I have the courage to do what he did? Did he do the right thing? What would have been the right thing to do? What if similar evil is already going on in the society where I live? Would I recognise it? What if the evil is inside my own soul?*

ASSIGNMENT

Decide how you want your story to end. Write a draft for the final paragraphs.

CHAPTER 14: VILLAINS AND MONSTERS

Almost every story needs an antagonist – someone who opposes the protagonist, often a villain or a monster. In Horror and related genres, the antagonist is important, and may even be the most fascinating character of the story. Spend time developing and showcasing this character.

HUMAN VILLAINS

When the antagonist is human (or human-like or formerly human) and evil, he's called a villain. He may be a serial killer, a cruel despot, a sexual sadist, a religious fanatic, a playground bully or a hypocritical schemer.

A great villain makes your story memorable, so spend time developing him.

<u>Clichés to avoid</u>

* The villain who is pure evil without redeeming qualities

* The villain who is evil without real reason

* Hot stinking breath

* Maniacal laughter - "Bruhahaha!"

<u>Motivation</u>

What does the villain want, and why does he want this? 'Because he is evil' is not a sufficient answer. Understand what drives this character to do what he does.

Depth

Give your story emotional power and depth by making the villain a complex person. He doesn't see himself as evil, but as noble, and in his view of the story, he is the hero.

He has a genuine good side – perhaps he saves endangered wetlands from destruction or protects children from abuse. He may even be capable of redemption... but doesn't choose this path.

You can give your Dark fiction even greater depth by creating similarities between the hero and the villain. They may come from the same background, possess similar skills, share the same ambition, may even fight for the same cause. But they have different ethical standards and use different means.

The more they have in common, the more depth your story gains. If you want to give your story a strong psychological element, consider this: The hero and the villain have similar good and bad parts in their psyche. The hero struggles against the evil streaks in his nature, while the villain fights against the good streaks in his.

Describing the Villain

* Smiles
The villain's smile can be chilling, especially if you describe it in detail. Don't just write, 'He smiled'. Instead write something like;
His lips curved and bared teeth.
The corners of her mouth turned up, but the smile did not reach her eyes.
Use this technique sparingly. The less often the villain smiles,

the more chilling his smiles become.

* Movement
Show how the villain moves – probably with slow, deliberate precision. The slower, the better – but take care not to overuse the word slow/slowly.

* Voice
Describing the villain's voice can make his dialogue chilling. You may want to use a simile here, comparing the voice to something dangerous or unpleasant, such as a cutting blade or a dentist's drill.

His voice sounded like...
He spoke with the coldness of a...
His voice had the ... tone of a ...
His voice was as sharp as a...

* Eyes
When describing the villain's eyes, the simile technique can be effective. Compare the eyes or their colour to something unpleasant or dangerous. The eyes may be
as dark and murky as a stagnant pond
as piercing as a pair of daggers
glinting like steel blades
the colour of frostbite
as cold as..
as hard as...

* Smell
Is your villain fastidious, slothful, vain? Mention what he smells of to give the reader a hint of his personality and lifestyle. Does he smell of peppermint mouthwash and Italian aftershave, of beer and stale sweat, or of garlic and axle-grease? The best place

to insert a sentence about the villain's smell is when he approaches the PoV character.

* Hands

The villain's hands are worth describing – especially the texture of their skin and the shape of their nails. This works well in situation where the PoV realises the villain's true nature for the first time, and also when the villain prepares to hurt the PoV.

MONSTERS

If the antagonist is an animal or animal-like creature, base its instincts and motivations on those of real animals. Invite the reader to feel pity for the beast by giving it a motivation that readers can understand on a human level – for example, to protect its young.

Reveal it Bit by Bit

Horror writers face a challenge that is rare in other fiction: once the reader has seen the monster, everything afterwards feels less scary. It is almost impossible to build up tension in the story after this initial encounter.

The way around this is to reveal the monster bit by bit, showing a different part each time, and delaying the full view for as long as possible. Perhaps only its roar or gnarl is heard at first. Then there's the smell. Later, a glimpse of scales or fur, then a claw or the sulphurous glint of an eye.

Keep it plausible

If your monster is a beast of your own creation, plausibility is another challenge. Keep it as similar to real animals as possible, even as you give it greater size, sharper talons, a bigger jaw and a more aggressive nature.

How did it come into existence? Here are some possibilities:
* A prehistoric animal, believed extinct – perhaps a dinosaur or plesiosaur - has somehow survived or been recreated from fossilised DNA.
* A mythological creature, believed to be non-existent – Cerberus, Hydra, Kraken, Minotaur - is discovered to be real.
* A new species, previously unknown to mankind, is found in an unexplored region.
* A real animal has become infected with a known disease – such as rabies – or an invented virus, and this changes the animal's behaviour patterns and makes it dangerous.
* A mad scientist has bred a new species to prove it could be done, but lost control over it.
* A ruthless government ran a programme for breeding monsters to use in war against the enemy, but the animals defeated their handlers and are now on the loose.
* A mutation occurred, perhaps as a result of chemical or radioactive exposure, changing the DNA of the foetus, and the resulting animal is a monster.

If the beast is one of a species rather than a mutation or an artificial breed, you need a reason why its existence has been unknown to mankind. It has probably survived in a remote region, perhaps in a jungle - where new species are frequently discovered – or in deep waters – where allegedly extinct species are sometimes found to still exist.

A major plausibility factor is size. Don't just take an ordinary animal and imagine a mutation fifty times its size, because their skeleton would not be able to support their weight. Outsize flying creatures are even less likely, because the wings could not carry their bodies. However, water creatures can plausibly have enormous size, because the water supports their weight. A 500-foot squid is more believable than a spider or eagle of the same size.

ASSIGNMENT

Write three sentences, each describing one detail of your villain or monster, to insert into different parts of your story.

CHAPTER 15: GHOST STORIES

Ghost stories appeal to a wider audience than most other stories: children enjoy them as much as adults, and even people who normally cringe at the thought of Horror fiction gain pleasure from a good ghostly yarn.

You can read your story aloud to your family and friends by the fireplace on a cold winter night, or to a formal audience gathered to hear an author perform her work.

PLOT AND BACKSTORY

All good Ghost stories consist of two tales. The first is the past tragedy which keeps the ghost haunting in search of atonement or vengeance. The second is about the person whose life gets thrown off course when the ghost intervenes.

The Ghost story needs more pre-planning than most other dark fiction, because you need to weave these two strands together.

The human's story which takes place in the current time is probably the main plot. The ghost's story is 'backstory', revealed perhaps in dialogue when the ghost talks, or in the narrative when the human researches the history of the place.

SETTING AND MOOD

You may want to choose a creepy location – a cemetery, a castle ruin, a dilapidated mansion, an abandoned mineshaft – or you can surprise the reader by placing the haunting in a setting that's not normally considered spooky: a bingo hall, a family car, a grocer's shop.

Most hauntings are tied to locations, especially the places where they lived, died or are buried. Old inns, WWII airfields and theatres are among the most haunted places.

A common plot for a Ghost story is this: a character hears about a haunted house, derides the superstition, and spends a night there to disprove the existence of the ghost. The ghost is real and so terrifying that the character is glad to get away with his life, and never mocks ghosts again. Although many fine ghost stories are built on this plot, it is difficult to come up with a fresh angle.

Ghost stories flourish when you create a creepy atmosphere. The following techniques work especially well for Ghost stories:
- Darkness
- Sound
- Chill

For instructions how to use these, see Chapter 9.

The mood of most Ghost stories is creepy throughout. Humorous Ghost stories are also popular.

CHARACTERS AND POINT OF VIEW

The ghost haunts because she needs something, and she can find no rest until this is achieved. What does she need? It may be something benign, such as revealing the location of the treasure to the right person, to make amends for an atrocity, or something terrible, such as exacting vengeance and killing the last surviving member of a certain family.

Who is this character? Why does she haunt? What does she need? What does she do to get this? In what way does this particular human hold the key to her fulfilment?

The human wants something, too – perhaps related to either the ghost or the place. What does the human want, why does he want it, and why is he trying to get it at this time in this place? If the setting is an abandoned building or a remote location at night, you need to give him a good reason to be there.

How does the human feel about ghosts? Does he believe in them? How does he feel about this particular ghost?

You can give the story depth if the needs of the ghost and the human are related, especially if the human is about to make the same mistake the ghost once made, or has a similar guilty secret. Ideally, the human grows as a result of the encounter, and becomes a wiser, better person.

The natural point of view for a Ghost story is the human who meets the ghost. However, you can surprise the reader by telling the story from the ghost's point of view.

ASSIGNMENT

Choose a location for your Ghost story. Decide why the ghost haunts this place, and what it wants from the human.

CHAPTER 16: VAMPIRES, WEREWOLVES, ZOMBIES

Vampires, Werewolves and Zombies feature in many Dark, Paranormal and Horror stories – perhaps also in yours. They are human – but not quite as we know it. Some aspects of their human existence are altered, paused or destroyed.

Although these entities are deeply embedded in the human psyche, perhaps even as part of the shared awareness Carl Gustav Jung called 'The Universal Unconscious', they have no single definite form.

Every generation has its own idea of what vampires, zombies and werewolves are like. Writers, painters, moviemakers and other artists keep reinventing them, giving them new shapes and characteristics. You are free to base your creatures on the tropes others have developed, or to interpret them in fresh ways.

Here are some guidelines as well as ideas how to twist them.

VAMPIRES

Although many cultures have folk legends of creatures drinking human blood, the real allure started when the vampire took human shape. This happened more recently than you may imagine. The first stories about vampires as we know them appeared in the 18th century, and were developed in the early 19th century.
In 1819, a young English doctor, John Polidori, with creative input from Lord Byron, invented the character of Lord Ruthven: an aristocratic fiend, immortal, seductive and dangerous. Polidori's suspenseful novella *The Vampyre* became a bestseller in its time. It's worth reading; you can download it free here: http://www.gutenberg.org/ebooks/6087

Although *The Vampyre* is almost forgotten today, it inspired other great early works of vampire fiction, including Bram Stoker's novel *Dracula*. Count Dracula became the archetype from whom most literary vampires evolved. Since then, authors have modernised, humanised and glamorised vampires. Every story presents a new image, continuing some 'rules' while discarding others and adding new facets. Authors Ann Rice, Laurell K. Hamilton and Stephenie Meyer in particular reinvented vampires.

Sparkling Versus Traditional

Some fans of the genre like their vampires creepy and dangerous in the tradition of Dracula, others enjoy the benevolent kind that sparkle in daylight. In some forums, heated debates rage about which are better and even whether both types actually qualify as vampires. Some readers would like to ban the old-style vampires, others call for an embargo on the sparkly ones. Don't let those arguments inhibit you. Just write about the kind of vampire you prefer, and if you like, you can even invent a new type.

Vampire Tropes

Although there is no standard vampire, certain features have become traditional. Your vampire probably has some – but not all – of these:

* is 'undead' in a state between living and dead
* drinks human blood (usually from the neck of a living, non-consenting human)
* has an adverse or strange reaction to sunlight (death, weakening, or sparkling)
* sleeps in a coffin

* needs to sleep on native soil, therefore carries some soil with him
* remarkably handsome
* seductive
* pale
* low body temperature
* Has two long retractable fangs
* averse to garlic
* averse to silver
* cannot bear the sight of a crucifix (or sometimes the sight of another religious symbol)
* suffers pain or injury when touched by holy water
* not reflected in mirrors
* cannot enter a home without being invited
* cannot cross a river (or sometimes no body of water)
* can hypnotise humans
* can impose his will on humans
* has superhuman strength
* has the ability to shapeshift (usually into a bat or waft of mist)
* can fly
* may be a loner or part of a hierarchical society
* immortal (or almost so)
* drains humans' life force to replenish its own
* can be killed with a wooden stake through the heart (sometimes also by decapitation, incineration or drowning)
* Vampires are former humans, 'turned' by a bite from a vampire
* When bitten by a vampire, a human weakens, dies or becomes a vampire

Pick, mix and match any of these features in your story, and use your imagination to create something new.

FICTION IDEAS

What if the victims give their blood willingly, in return for a boon? Is what the vampires offer a fair exchange for what they take? What if a human yearns for thrills, for immortality, for everlasting youth? What if she is willing to pay for this with her blood, her life, her soul?

What if it's the human who pursues the vampire to bring about that deal?

What if the vampire sucks not blood but other body fluids? Mother's milk, sweat, tears, semen? However, if the donor gives the liquid willingly, there may be no tension. In what way will the fluid theft harm the human?

What if the vampire sucks not a physical substance, but drains the victims of their emotional, mental or spiritual essence? What if the vampire needs the victim's courage, creativity, faith or love to replenish his own? Imagine a vampire's desperation as his own courage, creativity, love or faith is waning, and the only way to restore it is to steal this essence from another person.

What if a man married a woman for political reasons or money? He is unable to love - unless he steals love from other people, which he refuses to do. For forty years, she has been a loyal, loving wife who suffered deeply because she was not loved. Now she's dying a slow, lingering death. He wants to give her the love she deserves in her final months. Will he do it?

What if a woman needs courage to fight for, and protect her children? What if she's the only one who can save the children, but she's naturally timid? Since her teens, she's sometimes sucked courage from other people. She stopped doing it for herself because she considers it wrong - but what if it's the only way to protect her children from serious harm? What if there's some young macho male endowed with more courage than sense? Wouldn't it actually do him good to lose his foolhardy courage? It might even save him from lethal stupidities. Might the woman do two good deeds by stealing his courage to replenish her own?

What if a religious leader is a faith vampire? Whenever his own faith wavers, he sucks it from members of his congregation. On the surface, this is clearly a wrong thing. But there might be circumstances when it's 'right'. What if the strength of his faith has helped many others? What if the strength of his faith has been so inspiring that it gained new converts, that it healed the sick, that it led the Israelites out of Egypt, that it inspired thousands of others to choose the path of good over evil? There could also be more selfish motives. He's a bishop candidate and if his faith doesn't stand up to scrutiny, he won't get the appointment. He's a television evangelist and his faith has made him famous; he doesn't want to lose that fame. Or the income. And quite simply, he doesn't want to be without faith. His faith means so much to him. He remembers periods when his faith was low; they were hell. He suffered until he replenished his faith with someone else's.

With these concepts, bear in mind that the love, the courage, the faith would be real. Once the vampire has them, s/he would be filled with true love, true courage, true faith. They don't desire a fake; this isn't about pretence. This is about the real thing.

These are just ideas you could develop.

WEREWOLVES

Fiction about humans shifting into animal shape, usually wolves, dates back far in history. In ancient Greek myth, the god Zeus punished humans for their sins by turning them into wolves for nine years. In Middle Ages fiction, werewolves were often benign, aiding the knights on their quests. While wolves are most common, other animals are also possible. For example, African myths have a were-leopard.

Werewolf Tropes

Here are some common features of werewolves.

* Normally lives as a human, but turns into a wolf at certain triggers
* The full moon is a common trigger
* May be able to change shape at will
* Superhuman strength
* Possessive
* Jealous
* Loyal
* Dangerous
* Organised in hierarchical packs
* Lives an ordinary human life, keeps werewolf nature secret.
* Immortal or hard to kill
* Can be killed with a silver bullet
* A bite from a werewolf infects, and the bitten person becomes a werewolf

Questions To Consider

When a human changes into an animal, he may get a sharper sense of hearing and a much keener sense of smell. Bear this in mind especially when writing from a werewolf's point of view. You may need to switch to more sensory descriptions with emphasis on smell. The change also affects how he notes threats and how he reacts to them, how he responds to the sight and smell of blood, and how he fights.

Does the body mass remain identical? Is the wolf exactly the same size as the human? If not, what happens to the rest of the mass?

To shift shape, the body needs different organs and bones. Do the old bones break before they reassemble? Do organs shrink or liquefy before they are recreated? How long does the process take? Does the character stay conscious during the change? If yes, how does it feel? Perhaps it starts as a soft tingle and escalates into excruciating pain?

How does the human feel about his wolf existence? How does the wolf feel about his human identity? To what extent do they share an awareness? After changing, does the human remember what the wolf has done?

Can the human choose when to change, or is he helpless? Does it happen every full moon, or at other regular intervals? What if the change is triggered not by moon phases but other factors either within or outside of the character's control – solstices, planetary alignments, the weather, the menstrual cycle, lovemaking, sugar-rich food?

It's possible to cast silver bullets and to shoot them from a normal gun, as long as the size and shape of the bullets fits the gun, although tests show that silver bullets are less accurate than normal ones. Where would people in your story obtain silver bullets from?

ZOMBIES

Although flesh-hungry undead have been a feature of mythology since ancient days, for example in the epic of Gilgamesh, for most of the time there was no clear line between vampires and zombies. The fictional zombie as we know it is relatively modern, defined largely by George A. Romero's 1968 film Night of the Living Dead.

The word 'zombie' stems from the Haiti Vodun tradition, but was not widely applied to flesh-eating walking corpses until the second half of the 20th century.
While zombies still have physical bodies, their minds are irrevocably changed. No longer governed by a conscience, incapable of reason, unrestrained by values of right and wrong, they often follow primitive instincts. If their new focus is overwhelming hunger, they let nothing get in the way of their urge to feed.

How Zombies Are Made

Most fictional zombies have been infected by virus-spreading bites, often as part of a world-wide epidemic. Some were raised from their graves, either as part of a mass resurrection or individually, by necromancers, mad scientists or power-craving villains. A few have chosen the undead state for reasons of their own.

Zombie Tropes

Here are some typical features of fictional zombies. Some – but not all – may apply to yours.

* reanimated corpse
* mindless, cannot be reasoned with
* relentless, purpose-driven

* hunger for human flesh
* appetite for brains
* craving for salt
* retains some physical features and personality traits of the person they used to be
* body slowly rots, with parts dropping off
* sickening smell of rotting flesh
* keeps living in this undead state despite injuries that cannot be survived
* move in hordes
* besiege human dwellings

Fiction Ideas

Zombie fans can be fanatic about what is a 'real' zombie, and you can witness heated debates about whether 'real' zombies do or don't eat brains. Don't let these arguments restrict your creativity.

Confronted by a zombie, how will MC defend himself and those he loves?

What if the zombie is his friend, relative or spouse, with remnants of their old personality? Should he protect them or kill them?

Is a zombie an individual with human feelings and rights, or is it a menace to be destroyed?

Who would raise or create zombies, and for what purposes? A government needing an army of fearless soldiers? A greedy capitalist wanting low-cost labour for his factories? A scientist seeking to prove it's possible to assemble a new human from dead body parts? A dying person in search of immortality making a pact with a necromancer?

BEWARE BITE-HIDERS

Avoid this over-used plot device: a pair or group of survivors fight against the infected undead. At the critical moment, one of them reveals his fangs. He was bitten a while ago, but has hidden the infection from his friends. Now he attacks them.

For some reason, almost every writer of paranormal fiction seems to hit on this idea. Editors and fans are tired of this twist.

ASSIGNMENT

If you want to write a story about zombies, vampires or werewolves, study the list of tropes and choose the ones that intrigue you.

CHAPTER 17: RELIGIOUS HORROR

Religion and horror form a powerful partnership in fiction. Religion can bring out the best in a person – or the worst. Think of the crusades, conversions at sword-point, curtailed civic liberties, torture by the Inquisition and predatory paedophile priests, as well as the subtle dangers of bigotry, dogma and hypocrisy.

Horror fiction allows you to get across a moral message without sounding preachy. The readers are absorbed in the excitement of the tale and don't feel they're being lectured to. This makes them more receptive to your points.

You can use Horror stories to draw people's attention to ethical questions, guide them to spiritual insights, and make aspects of your religion memorable. If you wish, you can inspire your readers to probe their own conscience and examine their faith. You can raise questions about religious dogma, the modern interpretation of old rules, or the definition of sin.

HORROR IN HOLY BOOKS

Although I'm drawing on examples from the Bible in this section, you can apply the techniques to the holy books and sacred myths of other faiths.

The Bible contains a surprising number of dark, scary, grisly and disturbing tales.

You can use a straight retelling of a section from the Bible and flesh it out. The Bible language is mostly terse, summarising the events in a 'telling' style. By fleshing it out in a 'showing' style with literary techniques, you can let the readers experience what it was like.

Think of Jonah. First there's a terrifying gale and the danger of the ship sinking. Then the sailors toss him overboard into the stormy sea. And finally, he gets swallowed by a whale and survives for three days and nights in the fish's belly. Can you imagine a more horrifying ordeal? What would it be like inside the fish's stomach: the darkness, the sounds, the textures, the smells, the claustrophobia, struggling for air, with almost no hope for rescue?

Job's story is horror, too: calamities befall him, and when he thinks it can't possibly get any worse, another disaster strikes. His home is destroyed, his possessions are stolen, his children get killed, he is afflicted with a disfiguring disease and more. 'Fear came upon me, and trembling, which made all my bones to shake'. This line is from Job's story (taken from the King James version of the Bible), and it's pure horror.

Daniel is another character with a scary experience: his employer, King Darius, had him thrown into the lion's den. Imagine what that felt like: the hungry lions pacing around him, sniffing at him, exploring him as a source of food, the floor littered with the gnawed bones of animals they had eaten earlier, their growls, their hot foetid breaths...

This kind of story is particularly useful for drawing believers' attention to sections of the holy book, and to make those events real in readers' minds.

Alternatively, you can apply your storytelling skills in a more creative way. Write the stories the Bible only hints at but doesn't tell. Take the perspective of someone who suffered either human cruelty or God's wrath. What was it like to be trapped in

Gomorrah when fire and brimstone rained from the sky and destroyed the city and all who lived there? What was it like to drown in the great deluge, watching Noah's ark float away in the distance? How about a mother in Bethlehem, desperately trying to save her children after Herod ordered the massacre of all young boys in that region?

If you like, you can take this one step further and write from a point of view that does not share the Biblical perspective.

Perhaps your characters are bravely and desperately defending the walled town of Jericho against Israelite attackers to protect their wives from rape and their children from slaughter, which were the common fate of defeated defenders in the ancient world. Or you could write about an Egyptian family who suffered cruelly because Pharaoh refused to listen to Moses' warning, "Let my people go!" They watched the Nile on which they depended for their drinking water turn to blood, and were beset by masses of biting gnats. An epidemic wiped out their livestock, their bodies broke out in boils, a hailstorm damaged their homes, locusts devoured their crops, and then their firstborn children died. Or consider what it was like for a soldier in Pharaoh's army, obeying the command to pursue the Israelites into the area vacated by the parting sea, only to be swept to death by the returning waves.

With this kind of story, you can raise questions about divine justice, and make your readers uncomfortable.

FAITH VERSUS FEAR

When writing about religious heroes, especially biblical figures and saints, it may seem natural to show them as unwavering in their faith or courage.

However, the story becomes more exciting if you insert moments of doubt and fear for the hero to overcome. Indeed, the greater the hero's fear, the greater is the eventual triumph of his bravery. Let him waver in his faith and suffer doubt before he regains his spiritual resolve. This makes the hero human and real, someone the reader can identify with. The temporary doubt and fear will create enormous tension.

RELIGIOUS HISTORICAL HORROR

If you write Historical fiction, you may find many scary religious contexts.

The hero probably has modern attitudes of compassion and tolerance, while his contemporaries may apply religious rules in the rigid, gruesome ways of their period. You can handle this sensitively as a dark story that raises subtle questions about perceptions of right and wrong.

You can also write this as scary horror. When the hero tries to save a victim from the fanatics' wrath, he himself gets denounced as a heretic and tortured or killed.

The martyrdom of saints also provides material for scary, often gruesome stories.

UNBELIEVERS MEET SCARY GODS

The character explores an old temple or other sacred site, asserting that those gods don't exist, and committing an accidental or intentional sacrilege. Then he realises that the deity of the temple does exist, is angry and will punish him terribly. This simple plot can make a scary Horror story, especially if you use a creepy location, make the realisation gradual and have the character's friends turn their backs on him so he faces the divine wrath alone. For a more complex and harrowing story, the character's beloved companion may become the angry god's innocent victim. This story works well with real ancient religions, and also with invented fantasy religions. The character is probably an atheist who denies the existence of any god or spirit.

STORIES PRESENTING RELIGION AS EVIL

If you have a grudge against a specific religion - or against religion in general - you can use it as material for your stories. However, pure rants and hate-mongering make shallow fiction.

Instead of presenting the whole religion as evil, focus on the evil specific characters commit in the name of their religion. Individuals abuse other people's piety to misguide them for their own ends – often greed, power, or sexual gratification. Religious fanatics can be even scarier, because they genuinely believe that God wants them to carry out these atrocities.

To give these stories depth and emotional impact, let the hero and the villain share the same faith, but interpret it differently. If your hero doesn't follow the villain's religion, consider creating a minor character who believes the same things as the villain, but is noble and honourable, tries to stop the atrocities, and becomes the villain's victim.

WRITING ABOUT OTHER FAITHS

When writing fiction about a religion other than your own, you need to research the tenets of that faith. Don't rely on assumptions, hearsay and prejudice.

You need to understand that religion's messages and values before you allow your fictional characters to misunderstand and distort them.

CONTROVERSY

Fiction about religious matters creates controversy.

Ideally, your story will inspire readers to probe their conscience, search their soul, ask questions, examine their faith. The reading experience will help them grow and they will emerge a little wiser, purer and stronger. Readers who are secure in their faith may welcome the opportunity.

But others may feel threatened. They realise that uncomfortable questions may undermine their fragile faith, and they want to avoid that. At best, they'll simply avoid your story. At worst, they may rant against it and even call for the publication to be banned.

You may choose to ignore the controversy, or you may embrace it. You may even rejoice about the publicity and the consequent fame and income.

If you fear controversy, stay away from writing religious horror.

ASSIGNMENT

If the dark side of religion intrigues you, or if you want to get a spiritual message across, brainstorm some titles and add them to your list.

CHAPTER 18: WHY DO PEOPLE READ HORROR FICTION?

Fear, worry, revulsion, terror – in real life, we seek to avoid them. Yet in book form, they grant delicious thrills. What attracts readers to Horror fiction?

As a fan of the genre, I've found several explanations.

SEVEN PSYCHOLOGICAL REASONS

1. Escapism. Exciting stories distract us from the unpleasantness of real life. While reading, we become so absorbed that we forget about our everyday worries and the looming threats. More than most other genres, Horror fiction offers excitement.

2. Perspective. The suffering of fiction characters makes our own troubles seem less severe. The arthritic twinge in the knee and leaking roof which normally drive us crazy suddenly seem minor after we've spent time with characters who've had their legs ripped off and survived a snowstorm without shelter.

3. Adrenaline rush. In dangerous situations, the brain releases a cocktail of adrenaline and other chemicals into the bloodstream to give us the stamina and courage needed to face the threat. These chemicals induce a high – a mild one for some people, a powerful surge for others. Horror fiction provides the same thrill as real danger, but in complete safety. The pleasure is similar to that of bungee-jumping, and can be addictive.

4. Education. Horror stories teach valuable lessons about good and evil, about ethical conflicts and moral dangers, about unseen dangers and disguised threats. Sharing the fictional characters' adventures, we learn from their experiences, without making

their mistakes and taking their risks.

5. Reassurance. Many Horror stories – although not all – show that in the end, good triumphs over evil. Humans need that reassurance. In this respect, Horror stories are for adults what fairy tales are for children.

6. Personal growth. Story events put the fictional character's strength, resolution, ethics and courage to the test. As the character grows through experience, so does the reader. Dark stories invite readers to ask themselves what they would have done in this situation, to compare the character's courage with their own, to probe their consciences and explore their own ethics.

7. Control. By reading, we gain control over our fears, at least temporarily. Whatever scares us, we can face this danger in fiction, reading as much or as little as we like, and are able to close the book when we've had enough. This sense of control can be empowering, especially for people who suffer from phobias and irrational fears.

Think of the horror fiction you enjoyed – creepy ghost stories, shocking tales of violence, disturbing fantasy yarns – and about the ways in which they gave you pleasure.

ASSIGNMENT

Think about what kind of Horror fiction you like. What is it that makes Horror enjoyable to you? How can you create these elements in the stories you write?

CHAPTER 19: MARKETING AND PUBLICATION

When you have written your story, seek feedback from other writers, and revise it until it is as strong as you can possibly make it.

Then it's time to send it out into the world, so it can be enjoyed by many readers. You have two valid options – either go the traditional route and submit it to a publisher, or be your own publisher and present it directly to the readers.

TRADITIONAL PUBLISHING

Markets

The main markets for short stories are anthologies and magazines. While the print market is shrinking every year, the digital market grows rapidly. Your chances of placing your story in a printed magazine are small, but we've entered a golden age for electronic publishing, and there are many ezines buying dark short stories.

Look at markets (magazines, ezines, anthologies etc.) that publish your kind of stories. Study the Guidelines for Contributors on their website. What kind of stories do they want or not want? What topics, word count, style?

Submit your story only if it's a good fit for that publication. An anthology of Scottish Gothic Romance won't be interested in your Brazilian Splatterpunk, regardless of its merits. If the Guidelines for Contributors say 'No Vampires', don't bother sending them your vamp yarn. If the editor is known to be a homophobe, don't submit your story about lesbian ghosts. However, the statement 'no horror' sometimes means merely that they don't like gory fiction of the Splatterpunk and Extreme Horror type; they may accept Psychological Horror or Gothic Fiction.

The Guidelines for Contributors often say what kind of story the editor really wants. Take this seriously. Be the writer who supplies what the editor doesn't get enough of. This strategy can be the launch of your career as an author.

If your story is rejected, don't take it to heart. Most markets receive several hundred submissions for every story they publish. Your story may simply not be exactly what the editor wants at that time. Or perhaps the editor has recently accepted a similar story and wants to avoid repetition. Perhaps your writing isn't yet up to the demanding standards of that market. Simply send it to the next market on your list. Most writers receive many rejections before the first acceptances arrive.

Many markets have 'reading periods' during which they accept submissions. Outside those periods, submissions get ignored.

Some publications say 'no simultaneous submissions' which means you're not allowed to submit the story elsewhere at the same time, but have to wait for this editor's decision. This can be awkward if you have to wait for months before you receive a reply. It can take years before your story finally finds a home.

A good place to find markets is Ralan's Webstravaganza. It's a well-maintained online list of publications that accept submissions in Horror, Humour and related genres, searchable by pay scale, genre and other criteria, and it's free. http://www.ralan.com/

Rights

Be careful about what rights you sell. Ideally, you should keep all rights to your story, and merely grant the magazine the right to publish your story once. However, some markets require a period of exclusivity, for example, you may not publish the story elsewhere for six months. This is reasonable.

If a magazine demands 'exclusive use' or even 'all rights', beware. Agree only if the benefits are substantial, for example, if the publishers pay you a lot of money. You may want to seek legal advice before signing away your rights.

Payment

Payment varies greatly. Only you can decide what is acceptable, but here are some suggestions for your strategy.

At the beginning of your career, you may accept token payments because experience and exposure are more valuable than money. When you reach the level where you earn an income from your writing, you'll submit only to markets that pay professional fees. There are far more token-paying markets than pro-paying ones.

For a new story, payment is usually higher than for a previously published one. Professional writers earn their income from the first fee for their story. Payment for reprints is just a little extra. Sometimes, I allow anthologies to publish my previous stories free, because the exposure is good promotion for my books.

If a market offers to pay not in money but in 'exposure', think carefully. Quality exposure is valuable, but those markets are often not quality. Being associated with a low-standard publication is not helpful. At best, nobody will read that publication. At worst, it may harm your writing career.

I don't like telling writers what they should 'never' do... except in this one matter: never pay anyone to publish your story. That is called 'vanity publishing' and frankly, it's a scam. Many vanity publishing enterprises prey on gullible novice writers. Don't fall for their tricks.

SELF-PUBLISHING

Also called 'independent publishing' or 'indie publishing', self-publication has recently become a valid option for fiction writers. You are the publisher as well as the author.

Until a few years ago, self-publishing fiction was a foolish undertaking; only non-fiction books stood a realistic chance of success. But with the new technologies such as PoD (print on demand) and ebooks which require little capital outlay, this has changed drastically, so don't dismiss this option out of hand.

Indie publishing is not an easy path, and writers who self-publish as a shortcut to bypass the quality controls of traditional publishing, are in for a harsh shock. As an indie publisher, you are your own gatekeeper, responsible for the quality of your writing. Many indie-published books are not as good as their authors think.

You also need to learn business skills, because you'll be your own marketing manager, publicist, formatter, bookkeeper, editor, art director and more. Even if you decide to hire experts to do some of these jobs for you, the responsibility remains yours.

I have had many books traditionally published before I switched to indie publishing. My twenty most recent books – including this one, and several short story collections – are indie-published. As a trained publishing manager with many years' experience in the industry, this has equipped me with useful knowledge and skills. You probably won't have this advantage, so you need to find other sources of information. Listen to writers who have successfully self-published and learn from them.

You can be a 'hybrid author', a writer who uses both traditional publishing and indie publishing. With short stories, this is a practical strategy: First you sell your story to a magazine and earn a flat fee, then you publish it yourself as an ebook and earn royalties from every sale.

At the moment, short story collections sell better than individual stories, so you may want to wait until you have several pieces. Collections sell best if they have a clear unifying theme. Consider publishing a book with stories of urban vampire Splatterpunk, Gothic Fiction about cats, Dystopian Horror set in China, Christian Dark Historical Fiction or whatever topic inspires you. You need at least three stories; more is better.

TRENDS

Fashions change rapidly. One year, the demand for vampire literature is big, the next, zombies are all the range.

With novels, it would be foolish to chase trends because by the time the book is written, fashions have moved on. As a short story author, you can take advantage of trends, especially if you're a fast writer. If a new trend inspires you, go for it!

However, write only about what excites you, or your fiction will lack power and sincerity. Don't let anyone deter you from writing your passion. If people tell you that 'the market for zombie fiction is dead' or 'Splatterpunk doesn't sell', smile sweetly and write it anyway. Even if your story doesn't sell in the current market, it may become a huge success in a few years when the fashions change. Also consider that there are always specialist markets and niche reader groups. Your story doesn't have to appeal to the masses, just to the readers who enjoy this kind of fiction.

Here's a list of current trends I've observed. You may be able to incorporate some of them in your fiction. Bear in mind that trends change, and by the time you read this book, some of my suggestions may already be out of date.

* Flash Fiction
* Cross-Genre
* Humour/Dark Comedy
* Deep PoV
* Main characters with physical disabilities
* Animal companions

ASSIGNMENT

1. Visit Ralan's website and identify several markets publishing your kind of story. Study their Guidelines for Contributors. Make a list of at least five markets, with the most desirable one at the top.

2. If you consider indie publishing, think of a unifying theme for your short story collection.

CHAPTER 20: SAMPLE STORIES

Here are three of my stories, illustrating techniques from this book, with comments added at the end. You may want to read each story and form an opinion about it before you consider my comments.

SHORT STORY: BURNING

Supper was bangers and mash with mushy peas. Mum had promised me the glossy calendar photo for November - lambs frolicking around Camber Castle - but only if I ate up every meal this month. I disliked greasy bangers, I despised mash, and I hated mushy peas, but I wanted that picture, and it was only the ninth. Half-listening to my parents' grown-up talk about the need for a new church, I stirred the peas into the mash. Instead of becoming more appetising, the meal now looked like a vomit puddle around dog turds.

Pa's knife sliced a banger; fat spurted. His face shone with enjoyment. My brother Darren stuffed his mouth with mushy peas and smiled as if he liked the taste, which I knew he didn't. I wondered if Mum had promised him the picture, too.

Mum patted her freshly permed hair. "It's almost night." She stood up to pull the kitchen curtains against the approaching darkness, the way she always did during supper. This time she paused. "There's a lot of smoke. It looks like something's burning down by the old harbour. It glows. Holy Mother of Jesus, something's burning proper. It could be the Eversons' shop."

Standing on my toes, I peered out of the window. My breath fogged the cold glass. With the sleeve of my jumper, I wiped a patch clear, saw dark smoke spiralling toward the empty sky. A light glowed a half-mile from our house, like an orange-coloured glimpse of hell.

Pa put his fork down. "I'll go down the road and watch."

"Is it wise to get involved with this?" Uncertainty quavered in Mum's voice.

"I'm not involved." He stood up and took his grey hat and winter coat from the clothes hook on the door.

"Can I come?" Darren asked through a mouth full of blackened sauerkraut. "I've finished my supper."

Pa was already tying a grey shawl around his neck. "Yes, you can come, son." He paused, pointing his chin at me. "I'll take the girl, too."

Frightened by what I'd seen out of the window, I tried to protest. "I don't want to go. Please..."

An angry glance from Pa shut me up. His hard hand pulled me away from the table. "You'll come."

Within moments, Mum had bundled me into my anorak, a thick knitted shawl and a woollen hat. "Stay with Pa, don't catch a cold, and don't talk to anyone."

Darren grabbed his superman jacket and cap and ran down the stairs, and I followed. At least I had escaped from the mushy peas.

Pa forced me into the black metal seat on the bar of his bicycle, so that I was locked between his body, his arms and the handlebar. At seven, I was really too old to travel in the child seat, but he seemed to like holding me captive, and I did not dare suggest I ride behind him on the luggage rack. Darren followed on his own bike.

A few minutes later, we reached the blaze, and faced it from the safety of the pavement opposite. My heartbeat roared in my ears like a locomotive. The fire was real in its frightful intensity. Thick smoke oozed through the roof and curled into grey spark-loaded columns. Hot stink wafted in our faces.

"Smells like we're burning garbage," said a woman with silver spectacles and wrinkly skin. Others laughed; their laughter sounded eerie against the whine from the fire.

Many people had come to watch the house burn. Onlookers stood in small clusters, their hands in their pockets, their faces muffled with shawls.

My mouth was dry and tense; cold prickled on my skin, and I put my hand into my father's coat pocket to hold his hand. "I want to go home, Pa. Please."

"Watch." He grabbed my shoulders and turned me towards the fire. "Watch and learn. Learn about what happens to garbage."

I tried hard not to look, but the glow drew and held me. I knew the house: The shop on the ground floor sold magazines, lottery tickets, ice cream, my favourite Werther's toffee sweets and Mum's cans of mushy peas. Above the shop was a flat, and above that, an attic under a gabled roof.

The façade looked thin and vulnerable. The upper windows contained dark emptiness, and the bow windows of the shop screamed with orange heat. Everything looked black against this orange. The house reminded me of the lanterns we'd been making at school, black cardboard with rectangular cut-outs, with brightly coloured translucent paper behind.

I didn't mind the rows of mushy peas cans burning, but I regretted the Werther's toffee and the ice cream chest.

"Are they in there?" a young woman asked in a thin voice. She carried a small white dog in her arms and stroked it incessantly. She tilted her head at my father. "The Eversons and the Arabs aren't still in there, are they?"

"I've only just arrived. I know nothing."

"If they were at home, they'd have come out by now, wouldn't they?"

When he gave no reply, she turned to the tall bespectacled woman. "The fire fighters are taking their time, aren't they?" She stepped from one foot to the other, either nervous or cold. "They've been notified, haven't they?"

"Yes," the other woman said.

"Well, they're volunteers, I suppose they can't be expected..."

"No."

"Still, why..."

The sea breeze whipped the flames into further frenzy. In the distance, seagulls screeched.

"I don't know anything, so don't ask." The older woman turned away. The younger one stopped talking, and pressed her face into her dog's coat.

Not everyone was quiet, though. Darren had met up with other boys from his class. They hurled stones at the windows of the upper stories, smashing the panes the fire hadn't reached yet, chanting something about cleaning up the town. Their teacher stood by, and I expected him to call the boys to order, but held his hands folded behind his back and watched.

Within moments, the sash windows of the upstairs flat lit up at once like a garland of festive lights. Glass crackled and tinkled, a beautiful chiming sound, dotted with poufs and bangs. The smoke grew darker and thicker, turning dirty brown and charcoal black. Plaster blistered and peeled off the wall. Embers flew.

Wind blasted from the site and threw furious heat at us. My face felt like a roasting sausage, but when I averted it, the icy night air made my hair stand up.

Sirens howled, the dog yapped, and people made room on the pavement for a shiny police car. Two uniformed policemen jumped out and shooed people back from the site, including the chanting boys. Then they stood, inactive, hypnotised like the rest of us.

Now smoke seeped from the small attic window, then it lit up as if someone had switched on a hundred lights behind a red curtain. A collective "Aah," rose from the crowd. A couple of people started to clap, but stopped when a policeman threw them a stern look.

I wasn't sure what it all meant. I couldn't believe that people were trapped inside this boiling heat. I scanned the crowd for the woman with the white dog, but she had disappeared, so I asked the woman with the spectacles. "Are there people in the fire? Are they burning?"

"Of course not, dearie," she soothed. "The Eversons are away on holiday. They had a sign in the window, 'Closed until Monday 11th'. And even if there was someone in there, they wouldn't feel a thing. The smoke would get them first. So don't you fret." She fished in her coat pocket. "Here, have a sweet, dearie." I hesitated, because my parents warned me not to take sweets from strangers, but Pa had laughed with this woman, so maybe she wasn't a stranger, and it was a Werther's toffee.

"Come on, take it."

Fearing to offend by refusing, I croaked a thank-you from my dry throat and took the sweet, but put it into my pocket.

Now a red fire engine pulled up with blue flaring lights. Dogs and sirens howled. While the fire fighters opened the hydrant and connected their thick limp hose, the burning house roared like an angry animal. The night sky now appeared deep blue, cool and clean.

I heard one fireman question a group of men. "Anyone still in there?"

"Don't think so. The Eversons own the shop and live in the flat above; they're away on holiday."

"There won't be much left of their shop and their flat when they come back."

"They're insured."

In the meantime, two fire fighters with helmets had rammed the door and gone in, but came out within moments, signalling with large arm gestures.

The fireman standing near us translated. "The staircase has collapsed. Nothing we can do."

Flames leaped high in the air, glowing orange and yellow, red and lilac, and it was the most beautiful and most horrible sight I had ever beheld. In the midst of the tumult, I heard screams from the fire.

Around me, people mumbled and shuffled their feet.

"It's the wood," someone said. "The fire has reached the ceiling beams." Another voice replied, "That's right. Old wood always sounds like that when it burns."

A fat dog howled and strained at its lead. But the people just stood, spellbound by the spectacle. The rumble and roar of the blaze absorbed any further cries. Huge billows of smoke and flame erupted when the roof burnt through and beams and timber collapsed with a crash.

A few moments later, the fire quietened, showing what was left of the building. The floor between the ground floor and the first storey still held. Above it, all was gone, apart from a few sagging fragments of walls, and the timbers on each corner which flamed like giant altar candles.

"That house is lost for good," the fireman said. "All we can do now is stop the fire from spreading."

The acid sting of wet ash got into my nose and into my throat where it scratched and tasted bitter. As best I could, I shielded my face with the knitted shawl. Dancing ashes showered us like confetti from a carnival float.

As the fire withdrew further, the darkness grew silent and cold.

"Time to go home," Pa said to nobody in particular. "The children are getting restless."

By the time we got home, I was shivering. Although I needed to ask many questions, Mum packed me into bed and told me to be quiet and sleep.

All night images of fire plagued me, and I feared I would burn. The bitter flavours of smoke and fear clogged my throat, and I heard the sounds of crackling fire. My heart hammered and my body was bathed in cold sweat. Many times I touched the floor to check it for heat, afraid that the storey below was burning. Any moment smoke and flames might burst through and engulf me in hell fire.

In the morning, I was still upset. My hair stank of nasty smoke, and my head burnt from the uneasy night.

Mum put her hand on my forehead while we sat at breakfast. "The girl has a fever. You shouldn't have taken her out in the cold."

"You've been too soft with the children. They have to become tougher." He lit a cigarette and puffed. Normally, he didn't smoke at breakfast. The smoke curled and found its way into my nostrils.

While the others had bread with butter and blackberry jam, Mum served up bangers mash and mushy peas. In our family, sickness was no excuse for wasting food. I recoiled at the vomit-like stuff, no less repulsive after microwaving than it had been before. Mum sniffed, but not at the food. "Holy Mother, you stink. All three of you. The smoke is in your hair."

I sliced a banger with my knife, and watched the grease run and curl around the peas-mash heap. Darren spread butter and thick blackberry jam on his bread. I glanced at the picture of the jolly lambs and decided it wasn't worth it. If Pa left for work soon, I might get away without forcing the horrid stuff down. Mum sometimes waived punishments.

The letterbox rattled, and a plop told us that the newspaper had arrived. Mum fetched it. She moved the bread-bowl to the side and spread the paper out on the kitchen table, opening it on the first page of local news.

I read the headline, one bold word after the other. *"Family Perish in Fire - Hoax Call Leads to Destruction of Shop and Homes."*

Perish meant something like 'die'. But surely nobody had died. We'd been there, and everyone had said that the Eversons were away on holiday.

A large photo showed a smouldering ruin, a smaller one depicted fire fighters directing a blast from a hose.

Darren grabbed the paper and read aloud. "Three members of the Maqsoum family died in the fire. They were..." He mumbled the names and ages of the victims.

So people had died. They had burnt like the martyrs in the most frightening stories of *The Children's Book of Saints*. But it couldn't be true. The saints had died in faraway countries a long long time ago, not at the end of our road last night.

The report said that the local fire fighters had been called to a non-existent fire, which made them late to arrive at the site. It described how the charred remains had been found. The mother had cowered under a table while the father and the eight-year-old twin daughters had squeezed into a corner. The man was shielding the children's bodies with his own, apparently trying to hold off the flames from them until the last possible moment.

Nausea squeezed my throat again. These people had been awake and conscious. They hadn't passed out in the smoke, as the woman with the spectacles had tried to make me believe. With a pang of guilt I remembered the Werther's toffee I had accepted from her, and resolved to smuggle it into the rubbish bin later when nobody was looking.

I realised that the Arabs had seen the flames coming, looked into the deadly orange, smelled that bitter, acid smoke. Perhaps they'd found the exit blocked, but kept hoping that someone would get them out, if only they could retreat from the fire until help arrived. They'd withdrawn, shrunk into the corner, pursued by death. Even as the flames gnawed at them, as smoke clogged their nostrils and bit their throats, even as the flames started to devour their flesh, they continued to hope, even as the father sacrificed himself to gain a few more seconds for his girls... And then they screamed. I had heard those screams of pain and despair and death.

"They suffered," Mum said. "Holy Mother of Jesus, they must have suffered. I thought they'd go without pain, from the smoke. It doesn't seem right. Even for Arabs, this can't be right."

Pa shifted uncomfortably on the corner seat. I thought he would say something to praise the Arab father's courage. Instead, he lit another cigarette and said, "I'll be off in a moment."

Mum recovered and turned her attention to us. "Never play with matches," she lectured. "I've always told you so. Now you know what comes from being careless with fire."

"They were only Arabs," Darren said with the superiority of a twelve-year-old. "Dirty people. It was a dirty flat they lived in, full of clutter. Arabs live like that. I mean, just think of it. Four people in a one-bedroom flat. Decent people wouldn't live like that."

Although I didn't follow his reasoning, I accepted that the deaths had been at least partly the Arabs' fault, because of the way they lived, and because they had probably been careless with matches. I clutched my mug of hot milk.

"Why didn't they get out?" Mum wondered aloud. "They must have heard the fire, smelled something. They can't have been asleep at that time."

"Don't get involved." Pa took his coat and left.

Because of my fever, Mum made me stay in bed all day and brought me chamomile tea and hot water bottles. I sweated in the heat.

I could almost feel the hot breath of fire on my arms, and closed my eyes against the pain. In my mind, I crowded in the corner with the Arab family. We were trying to shield one another from the inevitable fire, the fear, the stinging leaps, the bites of the flames.

I thought of my own family. Strangely, I couldn't imagine Pa shielding us. I felt a yearning for the kind of love this Arab father had for his daughters.

In the evening, Mum made me sit at the kitchen table, either because she thought my fever had gone, or because she didn't want to annoy Pa. She plunked the plate of old food before me, not even bothering to reheat it in the microwave.

I was saved when a visitor came: the old woman with the silver spectacles. Mum patted her hair as if to check that the waves were still in place, and swiftly removed the plate with the disgusting food. Instead, she gave me and the woman fresh plates and we ate bread and mustard like the others. Of course talk turned to the fire again.

"Shame about the shop," the woman said. "I know Everson wants to move to more central premises where he can have a tea room, but it's still a huge loss."

Pa smiled. "They have insurance."

I didn't understand this grown-up talk, but had a vague idea that insurance prevented families from getting burnt. "Do we have insurance?" I asked.

"We don't need it. We don't have Arabs living in our house."

The mention of the Arabs made me cry.

"The girl's upset," the woman said. "It's been too much for her. She's so young. How old are you, dearie?"

"Seven," I managed between sobs. Then I asked the question I had wanted to ask all day. "Are they saints now? Have the gone to heaven?"

"No, dearie, they're Arabs. Arabs don't go to heaven."

I cried more. I wanted them to go to heaven.

Mum tried to console me. "Maybe there's something like a lower heaven where Arabs can go. Other heathens as well, if they've been good." She patted my hand. "Remember when your cat died? Maybe there's a heaven for cats and Arabs and other animals."

Darren giggled, and Pa snorted. "There's nothing in the Bible about that."

For a moment, all was quiet. Mum's mouth twitched like she might cry, too.

The visitor spoke into the silence. "If Everson doesn't rebuild, the site would suit our new church."

"We could use a new church." Relief sang in Mum's voice. "Something good is coming out of this after all." She folded her hands in her lap and smiled.

Pa and the neighbour smiled, too, because everything was good and right.

Comment

This is probably my best-known story, and it's one I'm proud of. I wrote it originally as an assignment for my masters degree in Creative Writing & Personal Development. It has been published in several versions and won contest prizes and commendations.

Is it Horror? Perhaps. Is it Dark? Definitely.

I compiled ideas with methods outlined in Chapter 1, drawing on my own fears: my phobia of fire, my nightmares of burning houses, a dreadful childhood memory of when my father forced me to watch a burning house, and my deep dislike of racial hatred and hypocrisy.

Then I used the freewriting method described in Chapter 3. This brought up events I had not witnessed, but heard of. One was when a house burned and the Turkish family who lived there had not been able to get out. Their charred skeletons told of how they had cowered in the corner as the flames devoured them, and the father had shielded his daughters with his own body for as long as he could. This moved me deeply, and then I heard someone say, "They were only Turks. Good riddance to the vermin."

The other was atrocities committed against Jews during the Nazi period. In the town of my birth, locals burnt the synagogue and then built a church on that spot. In a nearby town, the eager citizens went even further: they locked the Jewish population into the synagogue before they set it on fire. The fire brigade, instead of putting out the flames, fanned and fed them, and made sure none of the Jews could escape.

I wrote this as a Slice-of-Life story in Deep PoV, third person, from the perspective of a child who does not fully understand what is going on. The reader understands more than the PoV does.

You may notice how I described the girl's visceral reactions to what she sees and learns, and how I employed darkness to make the story frightening.

SHORT STORY: SEAGULLS

While the stencils dried above the dado rail, Josie squatted on the carpet, eating her first breakfast in the new studio flat.

Three seagulls stood outside the window, white-feathered and silver-winged, their eyes yellow halos around death-dark cores. Every time Josie lifted a spoonful of muesli to her mouth, their greedy stares followed her hand.

According to the *Welcome To Sussex* pamphlet, European herring gulls were an endangered species, worthy of protection. On the brochure's cover, seagulls looked so pretty: white-feathered, silver-tipped, soaring serenely in an azure sky.

In close-up reality, they were ugly, unromantic beasts, from the wrinkled flat clawed feet and the grey-pink legs to the folded wings ending in feathers like black blades. Each thumb-long beak had a hole in the upper half, some weird kind of nose she supposed, a gap through which she could see the misty sky. Then there was the red, a splash of scarlet on each beak, as if they carried fresh innards from a slaughter feast.

A sudden screech, and they dropped their pretence at peacefulness. Big beaks were pecking at her miniature roses, ripping them out and apart, tossing green fragments.

Josie stormed to the window, waving the tea towel like a weapon. Three pairs of wings unfolded, filled the window, lifted off. Screeches of outrage tailed off into the distance.

Of the pretty pink roses she had planted with so much care yesterday, only stems and shreds remained. With delicate fingers and tender words, she pressed the roots back into the soil and gave them water to settle back in.

She returned to work, sponging the next layer of stencils, delicate blooms in pink which would go well with chiffon curtains.

*

At noon, she left the stencils to dry and prepared lunch - muesli again, since she had not had time to stock her cupboard.

The gulls were back. Sharp bills pointed at the muesli on her spoon, begrudging her every bite. The one with deep grooves on its chin knocked its beak against the window. *Tap-tap, tap-tap.* More fiercely: *klacketeklacketeckacketeklack.*

The oat-flakes stuck dry in Josie's throat.

The tallest of the gulls, with head feathers standing up like a punk's haircut, tilted its head back and trumpeted a shattering scream. *Kreeeeee! Kreeeee!* The white chest vibrated with screeches which could have brought down the walls of Jericho. Josie wasn't sure if the window glass trembled, but the shudders in her spine were real.

The gull closest to her had obscene red stains on its beak, like a vampire's bloodied lips. Josie tried not to look, but she had to. Their closeness sent chills up her back, even with the transparent safety of double-glazing shielding her from predatory beaks.

If only she had curtains in place, preferably something as thick and solid as the garish seventies drapes she'd left behind in the shared London flat.

The red-billed gull unfolded its wings, increasing its size to fill the large frame, and more. Josie ducked behind two unpacked suitcases, but still their stares followed her. The studio flat, which had appeared so spacious when she had first viewed it, now closed in on her.

Living by the sea had seemed such a good idea, especially in St Leonards, where the streets hummed with history. She had pictured herself in a dress of sprigged muslin, strolling along the promenade on the arm of a Mr Darcy. A grey bombazine gown and a Mr Rochester would be good, too.

The gulls clucked like hens, trumpeted like elephants, screamed like pigs at slaughter, the noise shrilling through the window-glass and echoing in the unfurnished room. Why had they sought her out?

She scanned the houses on the other side of the road, Regency terraces with elegant wrought-iron balconies and bow windows on pale, ornamented façades. No unwanted visitors plagued those windows, although some seagulls socialised on distant roof gables and chimney pots.

Josie thought of squirting them with water from the plant mist spray, but living in cliffs, gulls were used to splashes, and of pelting them with hazelnuts from the muesli box, but they might just let the missiles drop off their feathers and gobble up the food.

Resolutely, she pulled her floaty velvet coat from a suitcase and threw it full force against the window. The big gull stepped back and dropped off the ledge, but within moments it was back.

Josie retreated to the windowless bathroom, where she emptied a jar of perfumed crystals, a farewell gift from her flatmates, into the steaming tub. Like always, the scent of lavender soothed her. During the hot soak, she was able to view the seagulls' behaviour as a mere annoyance, and her own reaction as ridiculous.

How strange that the birds homed in on her, and how strange that she was so frightened of them. After all, they were only birds, kept out by a double panel of solid glass.

But then, she'd always been frightened easily. As a child, she feared the neighbour's dogs, just because they were big and fierce looking, while young children patted them with fond trust. She could not bring herself to go near the farmer's cows, or the ugly looking turkeys in the cage. All harmless animals, of course, and only a stupid child would be afraid of them. The other kids made fun of Josie's fears, teasing her without mercy until she despised herself.

She covered her legs in thick soapy foam and shaved them with deliberate slow strokes, a reassuring routine, and stayed in the bath until she had used up all the boiler's hot water.

By the time she had rubbed her skin dry, the gulls had departed, probably to the beach to snatch snacks from unsuspecting tourists. In the bright sun, the glass showed zigzagging white lines where beaks dribbled, and white faeces gleamed on the windowsill ledge.

With the monsters gone, she browsed the mail order catalogue for curtains and furniture, designing light-filled, romantic space with swathes of chiffon and Regency prints, and pondered what to wear when she started her new job on Monday.

During supper - more muesli - , the same three gulls returned. *Klacklack klackeklack.* All three, hammering against the glass. Josie recognized the grooved throat, the blood-stained beak, the punk-style feathered head.

They knocked the window by moving their heads forward and back. Even ghastlier, the small one kept the tip of its upper beak glued to the glass, and vibrated the lower one. The whole pane rattled in an angry staccato. Josie had heard that bridges collapsed when a unit of soldiers marched in synchronised steps. Would the window break under the persistent pecking?

For the first time, she wished she was still in London, in the soulless grey tower block with views of other soulless grey tower blocks, in a flat furnished with someone's hideous nineteen-eighties leftovers, with flatmates whose unwashed dishes stank up the kitchen and whose stereos thumped through the night. The flatmates would know what to do, or would at any rate drown out her fears with their loud laughter and roaring rap.

"Oh, go away, go away!" she shouted at the beasts. Without the slightest shift of a leg, blink of an eye, twitch of a wing, they sat and stared.

She grabbed a fistful of muesli. "If I give you this, will you go?"

Kreeee-kreeeeeee. Kreeee. Impatient foot-tapping, as if they knew what was in the box.

She turned the squeaking handle, tilted the window, and dropped the muesli on the sill. They snatched the crumbs as soon as they fell, three scimitar-sharp beaks devouring the raisins and oat-flakes faster than she could dip her hand back into the box. *Kreee-kreee.*

If she gave them enough to fill their stomach, they would not bother hanging around. She grabbed another fistful and pushed her hand through the gap.

Pain shot like a piercing nail through her flesh.

She pulled her hand back, slammed the window shut and twisted the lock. Dark red blood streamed from the wound, dripping thick blotches on the pristine white windowsill.

The gulls yelled in angry triumph.

Having neither antiseptic nor a first aid kit, Josie rinsed her hand under the tap and wrapped it with an embroidered handkerchief. She needed allies, someone who had experienced this kind of harassment and knew what to do. But she had not yet introduced herself to her neighbours, and the harridan in the flat below had complained about the noise of Josie dragging suitcases up the stairs.

Dusk descended, but the gulls did not retire to roost.

Klackedekackedeklcackedeklack, they hammered at the window. Josie blessed the double glazing. Even if they cracked one pane, the second would resist, wouldn't it?

Josie scanned the other buildings in the evening mist. No seagulls were attacking the mock-Georgian retirement homes, the Victorian gothics, the concrete monstrosities from the seventies. Why had they picked her?

Maybe because she was at home when most residents were out at work. Maybe the absence of net curtains had lured them with a tempting view inside. Maybe they'd tried all the other windows, and learnt that they'd not get fodder there. She cursed her weakness of giving them muesli. Now they would not go away.

A soft, prolonged scratch. And another.

One gull was scratching along the edge of the window; the other two pecked at the putty that held the glass in the wooden frame. Josie had heard that great-tits and other songbirds sometimes nibbled at window-frame putty because they loved the flavour of the linseed oil it contained. Since seagulls didn't eat putty, what was their plan? If they pecked the stuff to loosen the glass from its frame, she would be trapped in a room with three violent seagulls hacking their beaks at her. What then?

Klackedeklack.

With her pulse thumping in her throat and ears, Josie put her door on the latch, and tried the flat next to hers, and the ones above, but nobody replied. The flats on the ground and first floors were still unoccupied after refurbishment. That left the one on the floor below.

Josie knocked and waited. A toilet flushed inside. At last, the door squealed open. "You." The sharp-nosed woman, with grey hair clinging like a steel helmet to her skull, stabbed a finger at Josie. "Do you know what the time is?"

"I, ahem…I know it's late, but..."

"Nine o'clock. Nine o'clock, do you hear?" Her voice whined like a dentist's drill, shrill, painful, persistent. "A time when decent people expect to be left in peace."

"My name is Josie Miller. I've just moved into flat six." Josie held out her hand.

The woman kept one arm locked across her chest, and with the second led a cigarette to her mouth for short angry puffs. "This is a respectable house. Or it used to be, until they refurbished and let the riffraff in."

"I assure you, I'm respectable, Mrs..." When the harridan did not supply a name, Josie said, "I'm a PA secretary at Lloyds TSB Bank, and the letting agent has my references. I'm sorry to bother you, but there are herring gulls by my window."

"In case you haven't noticed, this is the coast. Gulls live here."

"I'm just wondering how to treat them. I know they're a protected species..."

"Pests, that's what they are," the woman snapped. "Vile vermin, so don't feed them. Now excuse me. It's nine o'clock, and decent people have a right to peace."

The door clicked shut.

Josie checked her watch: eight forty-five.

*

She had to build a barrier. If she had furniture, she would push it in front of the window, and if she had tools, she would nail her blanket across. She managed to stand a suitcase on the inner windowsill, balancing her rucksack on top of it, filling the gaps with her still-wet towel and her winter coat.

Unless she held her hand very still, the pain was burrowing through her flesh. Holding the sponge for stencilling would be difficult tomorrow.

At least she no longer had to see the gulls. She lay on the carpeted floor, wrapped in her blanket, fantasising about a four-poster bed hung with drapes of rose-pink satin.

Klackedeklack. Scraaatch.

She turned on her CD player to drown out the seagull sounds. *Thada-thada-doum-thad.* The steady beat gave an excuse to her racing heart.

From below came outraged banging. The neighbour disapproved of the music. Josie plugged her ears with the iPod, but for once, the audio recording of Pride and Prejudice failed to absorb her. The fear in her stomach kept rising to her chest and throat, and she lay awake for a long, long time.

*

On waking, Josie's head ached and her throat scratched with thirst. She groped for the familiar lamp switch, and found only rough carpeted floor. Ah, yes, the new flat, and St Leonards, and the new job which had come up so suddenly.

Her brain felt like it had been boil-washed and tumble-dried. She stretched her aching limbs, scrambled up and stumbled to the window to pull the curtains back and let the dawn light in. No curtains, just a suitcase. Now she remembered: Seagulls.

When she undid the knotted hankie, she found the wound already healed over, the only slight discomfort coming from the tightness of the encrusted skin.

She lifted the suitcase away from the window. Sunlight bathed the room. Outside, cool dawn changed into a golden morning, and the distant sea sparkled like diamond-sprinkled satin. Nobody had ever been killed by a wild bird. A breath of the fresh, salt-laden morning air would drive the last of the childish scares from her over-tired head.

On the other side of the road, three white-feathered, silver-winged gulls sat squatting on chimney-pots, haloed by the morning sun, a picture of romantic innocence.

Josie turned the squeaking handle and threw the window wide open.

They rose, fluttered, soared...and then they were upon her.

Comment

'Seagulls' is my most reprinted story, published in many ezines and anthologies. The success always surprises me, because it's really a very simple story.

The idea came to me when I at my laptop, looking for an idea, and gazed out of the window. I live on the Sussex coast, and herring gulls are a major pest. Sometimes they sit on the windowsill, peck at the glass, and stare with menace. They can be dangerous.

The story is in third person Deep PoV. Observe how I isolated the main character and shut her off from all means of support, and how I used a trough (starting with 'Josie retreated to the windowless bathroom...') to manage the tension.

SHORT STORY: ONLY A FOOL

The *clack-clack-clack* of your heels echoes through the night-empty street. The drizzle paints needle-streaks in the light of the fake Victorian lamps. Already, the pavement grows slippery with roadside rubbish, rain and rotten leaves. You should have called a taxi while you had the chance. Now it's too late. Around here, the payphones are vandalised.

You stop to consult your *London A-Z* in a street-lamp's jaundiced glow, bending low to shelter the pages from the rain. The map suggests a shortcut. If you turn left into that alley, zigzag through the lanes, cut across the wasteland, you'll get home in under an hour.

Once you walked past that waste ground in daylight, and didn't like it. At night, you'll like it even less, but the drizzle thickens and creeps into the toes of your patent shoes. Why did you have to stay on at the party until after the last bus? Stupid woman. Better get home now, fast.

You dip into the gap between the dark façades. The alley smells of rotten fruit and piss. Two shattered windows wink.

Darkness folds around you.

Steps follow behind you in soft squeaks. When you glance over your shoulder, a figure squeezes against a wall, as if hiding from your sight.

You're a fool. Only a fool parties until after the last bus. Only a fool hesitates over the cab fare. Only a fool reveals ignorance by looking at a map. Only a fool walks alone into an unlit alley.

Fool, fool, fool.

You walk faster. Your heels echo louder, and your heart hammers in your ears. *Da-boom, da-boom, daboom-daboom-daboom.*

Your pursuer's squeaking steps resume, get closer.

You're too stupid to live alone. Didn't Paul tell you so? You should have listened to him, fool.

Keeping your stride, you grope through the tissues and tampons at the bottom of your bag, searching. Only a fool carries her personal alarm out of instant reach. Only a fool forgets her mobile phone at home.

Men always scent the victim smell about you. Lovers and strangers alike, they home in on you like wolves on easy prey.

Paul used to beat you, bruise you, break you. He told you that, despite your protests, you really enjoyed it.

Only a fool would have put up with it for seven years.

Seven years of fearing your husband's touch. Seven years of shuddering in meek endurance. If only you could have turned tables just once, let him taste the horror and the pain. But a nice girl doesn't fight, and a good woman keeps her mouth shut. Then the discovery of the catalogue, of the items he had marked: The nipple clamps, the torture racks, the chain floggers with skin-tearing hooks. Knowing he planned to use them on you.

Escaping that marriage left you without protector, vulnerable. Paul would not have let you go out alone at night. With him, you would not have walked into this trap.

Walk faster, now. Take bigger strides. Out-march the imagined danger.

Your arm is grabbed. You're slammed against the wall. Hard. Both hands pinned above your head.

A pimpled face leers down at you. Young. His breath smells of mint and beer. Your pulse pounds, and your tongue tastes fear.

When you squirm in his grip, rough brick chafes your wrists.

His thigh presses against yours. A knife at your throat, its edge a cold line across your neck. "Don't move."

You squeeze against the wall, into it, to get a fraction further away from the knife. Why did you not sign up for that self-defence class?

"Now pull up your skirt. Take your tights off. Your knickers."

The attacker pants. "But slow. Or I'll cut."

"No," your voice croaks, from far away. Then, stronger: "No. You wouldn't like my kind of sex."

Where did those words come from?

The edge leaves your throat. The grip on your wrists slackens a little.

Perhaps your attacker is not a seasoned rapist. Perhaps he's a boy trying it out. If you play this right, you may get away.

Perhaps.

"What kind of sex?" His eyes glint. "Why wouldn't I like it?"

You search your fear-paralysed brain for the reply that will buy time. "Few men have what it takes to please me."

For three heartbeats, his mouth stays open. Then a tongue wipes his lip. "Really?"

The grip around your wrist loosens more. The blade rests inches away from your throat. What caused this change? How can you use it?

His grin widens. "I knew you were different from others the first time I saw you." Leer. "A dominatrix. With leather gear and whip?"

Scheherazade used to spin yarns to save her life. Improvise. Quick.

"I wear black boots. Shiny patent leather. They reach up to here..." You expect him to release your hands so you can show, but he doesn't. Keep talking anyway. "Up to my thighs. With very high spiky heels."

He leans closer again, licks his lips. "What kind of whip?"

Paul's catalogue. The images. Remember. "Black suede. Thirteen long lashes. A plaited handle with silver studs. It sings and sizzles through the air before it thuds on your skin. Then there's a sharp sting..." The fantasy comes surprisingly easy. "But I don't sully my precious flogger on a dirty boy like you."

"Hey, why not?" He steps back. "Just because…"

"Precisely. Because." Your hands are free now. But to be safe, you must not run yet, must play the role a moment longer. "You don't deserve it. You have not earned the kiss of my whip. Nor the..." Scan your memory for images from the hateful catalogue. "The dog collar, the handcuffs, the cane..."

"The whip. Please." His eyes gleam with need and hope. "Let your whip kiss my arse. I'll be good."

Can this change be true? The pleasure of power tingles from your fingertips to your toes, invigorating every cell of your flesh. The strong animal in you, suppressed for so long, longs to burst from its cage. No longer a passive victim, now you can be in charge.

Purse your lips, as if assessing his potential. "If I give you a chance to redeem yourself, will you show me respect? Will you obey my will?"

"Yes, yes!" The eager face of a dog begging for crumbs.

"Then..." You stab a finger at his chest. "You will stay here, waiting, while I fetch my lovely, leathery whip. I'll test you, and if you're good, I'll let you feel its caress."

The pimply face lights. "I know a great place where we can go, not far from here. Behind the old cable factory. Nobody ever goes there."

Time for a stern frown. "It is I who choose the place."

"I go where you command."

"Stay here. Practice kneeling. Because when I come back, you'll be kneeling a lot."

Before the fool sees he's been duped, you stride off with power in your steps.

Your blood pulses. You're safe, and fuelled with new power. You've taken charge. No longer the victim. No longer the fool.

Of course you will not come back.

Why should you? Just to get another taste of this tingling power surge? Just to teach this boy a lesson that all males should learn? Just to punish him for all the abuse you had to suffer from men?

There's rage pounding through you, too. Rage at Paul who

abused you for years. Rage at men who attack women in the street. Rage at men who treat you as a fool.

The boy will be waiting. At your mercy. He'll go where you want, even to that deserted waste ground, and better still, to that place where nobody ever goes. He'll undress at your command, he'll kneel, he'll hold up his hands to be tied and open his mouth to take the gag.

Is this what Paul felt, this lust to hurt? It feels surprisingly good. The long-suppressed part of you cracks its chrysalis.

What will it feel like to slice a knife into those pale cheeks? To peel off his skin. To let his warm blood trickle over your hands. How soon will the scents of blood and fear outgrow those of beer and mint? To see the fear in his eyes. Uncertainty first. Then fright. Panic. Terror. Knowledge of death.

Will you give him what he deserves? What all men deserve.

Nobody knows who he is going to meet, so his body, when finally found, won't be linked to you. He's the perfect first object for your vengeance.

Only a fool would let this chance pass by.

Comment

This story started with the memory of a real incident. As a young woman, I lived in London. One night I was walking home from the Tube station when a drunken man molested me, and I was saved by my wits and vivid imagination. Over the years, I wrote and abandoned several stories based on the experience. Finally, I decided to make it a Horror story, added the BDSM subtext, hit on the idea for the ending, and the story worked.

The story uses Present Tense and second person Point of View. Both are unusual in fiction and seldom work, but for this story, they felt right.

Notice how I used several of the techniques described in Chapter 9: isolating the main character, darkness, sounds and visceral responses.

SHORT STORY: THE DEVIL YOU KNOW

Lucie clutched the pole by the exit, willing the train to go faster, urging it to take her further away from Jake.

"May I see your tickets?" singsonged a male voice. "Tickets, please."

While the seated passengers dug into pockets and rummaged through bags, Lucie reckoned she had about two minutes before she was found out.

She was in luck: the train slowed and hummed to a halt. She pushed the 'open' button and jumped out.

The place was dark and deserted, one of those small unstaffed stations. Behind her, the doors beeped and whooshed shut. The train accelerated with a growl and vanished into the night.

A rust-streaked sign proclaimed that she had reached Seelsden: merely five villages from where she had left. Her heart was still thudding from her escape, her mind reeling from the confrontation with Jake, and her thoughts churning in a jumbled mess, but she knew she had to hop onto the next train and this time try to get further.

In the sickly light of a wall lamp, she scanned the time-table poster. Only one train served Seelsden at night: the 11.36pm that had just rumbled away. After that, no trains stopped here until 6.42am.

The small station building was unlit, the door to the waiting room locked. At the contact point - 'For Information And Enquiries, Press Here' - a cardboard sign said 'out of order'.

She hugged herself against the chill and rubbed her bare arms. Now what?

An empty coke can rattled across the concrete, a crisp wrapper rustled along the track, and somewhere in the distance, a motor whined.

The hamlet of Seelsden was a mile away on that gloomy hill. A lone female trudging up there would put herself at risk from motorised predators, and even if she got there, where would she go? She had no money for a hotel – assuming that the village had one, which was unlikely. Other doors would remain locked. People around here did not open the door to strangers after 8 pm, and those who did had unsavoury intentions.

It was safer to stay on the platform, a semi-public place where she could see anyone approaching.

Overhead lamps soaked the station platform in their sulphurous light. The station clock ticked 11.50.

Claws of tiredness spiked at her brain. A warm bed, a cosy duvet, a safe place to spend the night... but there were only the benches along the single platform, with their hard white metal and curving backs. One of them would have to do for the few hours until dawn. She did not need to be comfortable, she just needed sleep.

Lucie picked the one least soiled by pigeon droppings and grime. The metal was cold, and the chill seeped through the thin fabric of her dress into her flesh.

It had been stupid to run away unprepared. She should have kept a bag packed, saved some money, identified places to stay. Instead, she had clung to her denial and her hopes that Jake would mend his ways, until she had no choice and she had to flee without even the chance to grab a jacket.

The jaundiced lamp glowed its disapproval.

If she had had any sense, she would have seen the danger signs as soon as she moved in with Jake – the satisfied pleasure with which he crushed that moth, the way he kept the spider trapped in a glass for weeks before he squashed it, the way his blue eyes gleamed when rough bedroom games escalated in violence – but she had clung to her denial, had shut out the truth even when it banged on her mind and demanded entry. Until tonight, when he had tried to...

No. She would not think about that.

She wanted to curl into a ball with her knees against her chest to keep warm, but the bench was too narrow for that. Cigarette stubs crammed into the gaps still stank of nicotine.

Denial followed by panic - this had always been her mistake. She could see the pattern now. When the lycée discriminated against girls, she meekly accepted it – and then one day she dropped out. When her father's new wife made her life hell, she suffered in silence – and then ran away. When the father of the family where she worked as an au pair made lascivious remarks, she ignored them, but when he tried to paw her, she freaked out, packed and left.

Each time, she could have made a formal complaint, given notice, taken her time to find a better way out. But each time she had denied, then panicked, and each time she had landed in a worse mess.

Midnight. Clouds flitted like pale ghosts across the sliver of moon. In the thicket that flanked the platform, rodent feet scurried.

She had to get some sleep. Dawn would bring warmth, light and clarity of thought.

Not far away, an animal howled. There were no wolves in England, she reminded herself. It had to be a dog. She turned to find a position of acceptable discomfort, one arm under her head and the other across her eyes, blocking out the light.

She woke, shivering. After a moment's disorientation, she realised where she was, and why. What a stupid situation to get into! At least it was over. But wait: the station clock said 2.13 - still four and a half hours before she could get into a train.

A pair of yellow eyes stared, flickered, vanished. There, again. Did England really have no wolves? Hadn't she read somewhere about wolves and foxes spreading into towns? And then there were exotic illegal pets, and big cats escaped from zoos.

Her pulse pounded in her throat. What if it was a hungry panther in search of easy prey? A thousand ants seemed to crawl over her skin.

Why hadn't she stayed on that train? Why hadn't she stayed at home?

Silence. Wind swished through the treetops.

She needed to go to the loo, really bad. But the railway companies had closed station toilets. Cost saving, budget cuts.

Another four hours before the train would take her away. And then, what? She still had no money, still had nowhere to go.

At least, the train would have a toilet. Probably. But could she hold out until then? The pressure on her bladder increased. Sleep wouldn't come back until she had a pee.

She squatted by the metal fence at the edge of the thicket, releasing a hot stream. Nothing stirred in the undergrowth. No eyes, no animal. She had imagined things because of her overwrought nerves. Already, she felt better. Even her panic about Jake subsided, and her thinking grew rational.

Running away like this had been stupid. If she had held out just a few more hours, she could have left in the morning with her clothes, with some money, with a proper plan.

Had she submitted until his violent lust was spent, she would have some bruises, but she would be lying in her own bed, cosy and warm.

Silly panic. How could she have thought Jake would kill her? He had different erotic tastes and sometimes he got carried away, that was all. She should have talked with him about her concerns and explained that they were not compatible. They could have had a rational discussion and broken up civilly. No need to panic, no need to run like a madwoman, no need to spend the night on a platform bench.

Those eyes again. And a second pair. Lucie's breath stalled, and fear clenched like a tight fist around her chest.

If only she had a weapon! That empty coke can over there – but it wouldn't help much even if she could reach it.

She lowered her lids, hoping this made her own eyes less visible to the beasts. But they had probably already taken her scent and were waiting to pounce. Would the metal fence keep them out? The bars were a handspan apart; too narrow for a big animal to squeeze through, she hoped. Another five minutes ticked by. Six.

She tried to hold absolutely still, so the predators would not see her move. How ironic: by fleeing from Jake, she had put herself in real danger. Instead of beaten by an intemperate lover, her flesh would be ripped by wild beasts.

If Jake were here, she would not be frightened. He would chase away the beasts, real or imagined.

A motor vroomed down the road. Twigs cracked, and when she opened her eyes a crack, the four gleaming pupils had vanished as if they had read her thoughts.

Where were the eyes now? Did she dare hope they had left? She breathed into her abdomen to still her racing heart. If she could get through the night, she would be more sensible in the future. She would talk things through with the persons concerned. No more rash running.

The night grew colder still, and the station clock seemed

paralysed, taking an eternity to advance by even one minute.

Wind rustled the leaves in the thicket, and the bushes seemed filled with flickering eyes - a trick of the moonlight glinting of pale leaves. As usual, she had overreacted, worked herself into a pointless panic. She had to get a grip on herself and stop indulging in silly fears.

Tiredness gritted her eyes and blocked her thought, and she must have slept, because when she looked again, the clock stood at 3.04. The bench had grown harder still, and the temperature had dropped beyond what any human would willingly endure. She rubbed her feet, trying to massage life into her icy toes.

Faint nausea rose from her stomach, and a headache threatened to split her skull. She remembered the week when she was ill, too sick to leave the bed. Jake had taken care of her, feeding her dry toast and sips of water, washing her limbs, emptying the vomit bowls, all with an angel's patience and a lover's tenderness.

A motor stuttered to a halt, a car door slammed.

Her mind raced through scenarios in which someone would drive to a deserted railway station where no train stopped at night. None of them was reassuring.

Heavy steps thudded on the tarmac, came closer.

It was best if the person did not see her here. She squeezed tighter against the curved back of the bench, the icy metal pressing into her cheek.

Thud, thud, thud.

Bunched keys jingled with every harsh step.

"Lucie?"

Jake! A warm wave of relief swept through her.

"Thank heaven, I've found you. I've searched everywhere." The familiarity of his firm, gentle voice enveloped her.

His shirt was unevenly buttoned, and stubble shadowed his jaw. He slipped off his leather jacket and draped it over her shoulders. "I've been worried sick. In the car, I have a thermos with hot tea."

She followed him out of the station gate to the car park. "I'm sorry I overreacted. When I saw that rope... I thought.. I panicked..."

"It's my fault, Lucie," he said gently. "I should have

explained what I was doing. Of course you were frightened. We need to talk. But first, I'll take you home. You look like you could do with some sleep."

He held the passenger door open and waited until she had sunk into the seat. The familiar smells – pine air freshener, fish and chips, milky tea - hugged her with their familiarity. Her mind sank into drowsy warmth.

Their relationship was doomed, she would tell Jake that. But she appreciated the trouble he had gone to in order to find her, and she would tell him that too. In her own time. No rush.

He got in on the driver's side, pulled his door shut, and snapped the central locking.

"Look at me, Lucie." His blue eyes gleamed, and his smile bared teeth. "See what I've brought."

His hands held the thumb-thick rope.

Comment

This story started with the memory of a night I spent as a young woman on a platform at Richmond station, waiting for the morning train to take me home, trying to sleep while the cold from the metal bench seeped through my thin dress. I kept the bench but moved it to an imaginary railway station on the Kent-Sussex border. Many of the small railway stations these days are unstaffed most of the time, with the waiting rooms and toilets locked, and the help points are often out of order.

Notice how I isolated the character, depriving her of any potential source of help. Also observe how I used descriptions of sounds, temperature and light to create a creepy atmosphere.

DEAR READER

Did you enjoy this book? Consider posting a brief review wherever you bought the book, have an account or are a member. Share what you liked most, what you liked less, and which story is your favourite. I value your opinion.

Reviews on sites like Amazon, Barnes & Noble, GoodReads, BookLikes etc. are very welcome. Email me the link to your review, and I'll send you a free review copy (ebook) of one of my other Writer's Craft books. Let me know which one you would like: *Writing Fight Scenes, Writing Scary Scenes, The Word-Loss Diet, Writing About Magic, Writing About Villains, Writing Short Stories to Promote Your Novels, Twitter for Writers, Why Does My Book Not Sell? 20 Simple Fixes.*

Do you know other writers who might enjoy this book? Tell them about it.

If you've discovered any mistakes, typos or formatting glitches, please contact rayne_hall_author@yahoo.com, so they can be fixed. Some errors may sneak past the proofreaders' eagle eyes.

On Twitter, https://twitter.com/RayneHall and if you tweet me that you've read one of my books, I'll follow you back.

I wish you great success with your own dark stories. Perhaps one day you'll be a famous writer, and when interviewers ask about the secrets of your success, you'll smile mysteriously and say, "I learnt many of my techniques from a book by Rayne Hall." I look forward to that day.

Rayne

ACKNOWLEDGEMENTS

I've had the help of several writers: Alicia McCalla contributed one of the ideas that got me started. Mark Cassell, Douglas Kolacki, Larisa Walk, Jonathan Broughton, Daniel Hinsley and William Wilkins each gave feedback for parts of the book. Thank you all!

Erica Syverson created the book cover and Julia Gibbs proofread the manuscript.

OTHER BOOKS IN THIS SERIES

More books are coming soon.

CPSIA information can be obtained at www.ICGtesting.com
Printed in the USA
LVOW10s1409070616

491586LV00041B/553/P

9 781499 324891